J.A. Hardgrave has written meant about a coming judgment. For many people, the Olivet Discourse is thought to be a prediction about the end-time judgment of our time. "Jesus is coming soon...The signs of the end are all around us...Come Jesus and rescue us from the mess of this world." There is a long history of this claim. Is it possible that many prophecy prognosticators have misread Jesus? *Jesus Wins* shows that Jesus won the victory long ago. He predicted events that would take place before the generation of His day passed away, and like the prophet He was, they came to pass as He said they would. If His word about events that happened nearly 2000 years ago came to pass as He said they would, then we can believe everything Jesus said, from His love for us to His victory over the world, the flesh, and the devil. *Jesus Wins* may startle you at first, but as you read on, you will come away with a greater faith in the reliability of the Bible and the faithfulness that is Jesus. And when you finish reading it, pass it on to friends to encourage them.

Gary DeMar
Author of *Last Days Madness* and *Wars and Rumor of Wars*

It is understandable that people can get very defensive when a belief they hold is challenged - because it shakes their whole world-view and causes them to question the views of the people who formerly taught them, people they hold in high regard. That's why theological debates usually produce very little change in opinions. What Jordan has done with this book is to take the topic of Bible prophecy out of the arena of debate and into the real-life journey of faith that all Christians are on. By showing us his own journey of discovery, his own conversations and learning experiences, and the conclusions he arrived at, we are able to lay aside our defensiveness because we can relate to Jordan's journey. I hope this book inspires you to make your own journey of discovery, and helps to lead you to the conclusion that the future is bright, God's Kingdom is advancing, and Jesus Wins!

Dr. Martin I Trench
Co-Author of *Victorious Eschatology*
www.martintrench.com

I am writing today not only to endorse the book Jordan Hardgrave has written, but to endorse the man. I have known J.A. Hardgrave for a number of years now. In this time, I have watched him study to show himself approved. Jordan, in his faithful diligence to God, to His word, and to the pursuit of revelation and spiritual understanding for proper application, present day truth is here. Out of his chosen obedience, God's will is being fulfilled. This book is challenging, enlightening, even humorous, but filled with present day truth. Jordan has penned life on each page. I hope as you read, you are not just taught, but become transformed as you glean from his teaching gift. It is through his God given ability that his words on these pages will give you opportunity to allow the anointing to be your teacher. Jordan, thank you for the honor of reading your manuscript and endorsing a young man I call friend.

Clay Nash
Author of *Relational Authority* and *Activating the Prophetic*
www.claynash.org

The book "Jesus Wins" written by J.A. Hardgrave brings a fresh perspective to this subject and is very well written and thought out. I love the dialogue between he and his mom, and that is relatable to nearly any age or background. I whole-heartedly endorse this book and encourage anyone interested in the subject of eschatology to give this a read. I would also encourage pastors and leaders to not only read this book, but also use it as a bible study tool to help others discover another way of looking at this subject in a non-combative way. The glorious truth is that the world is getting better and not worse. I believe it's time for us as the church to let go of any end time view that mirrors the story of Chicken Little and adopt a victorious and hopeful end time view that removes fear and releases hope to the generations to come.

Bishop Jamie Englehart
President/Overseer Connection International Ministries Network of churches

There is nothing else quite like the book you are holding in your hands. Here we have eschatology, one of the world's most controversial subjects, presented in a good-natured, easy-to-read conversational style detailing one man's personal journey through a mine-field of confusion towards mind renewing truth. A great work. I personally can't wait to see what else J.A. Hardgrave has up his writing sleeve.

Colin MacIntyre
Teacher and Graphic Designer
Creator of *Better Covenant Cards*
www.bettercovenant.cards

JESUS WINS
The End Times
Are Better Than You Think

J.A. HARDGRAVE

ISBN 978-1-64191-673-8 (paperback)
ISBN 978-1-64349-157-8 (hardcover)
ISBN 978-1-64191-674-5 (digital)

Copyright © 2018 by J.A. Hardgrave

All rights reserved. No part of this publication may be reproduced, distributed, or transmitted in any form or by any means, including photocopying, recording, or other electronic or mechanical methods without the prior written permission of the publisher. For permission requests, solicit the publisher via the address below.

Christian Faith Publishing, Inc.
832 Park Avenue
Meadville, PA 16335
www.christianfaithpublishing.com

All Scripture quotations, unless otherwise indicated, are taken from the Holy Bible, New International Version®, NIV®. Copyright ©1973, 1978, 1984, 2011 by Biblica, Inc.™ Used by permission of Zondervan. All rights reserved worldwide. www.zondervan.com The "NIV" and "New International Version" are trademarks registered in the United States Patent and Trademark Office by Biblica, Inc.™

Scripture quotations identified NLT are taken from the Holy Bible, New Living Translation, copyright ©1996, 2004, 2007, 2013, 2015 by Tyndale House Foundation. Used by permission of Tyndale House Publishers, Inc., Carol Stream, Illinois 60188. All rights reserved.

Printed in the United States of America

CONTENTS

Foreword 11
Preface 13
Chapter 1. The Left-Behind Series 17
Chapter 2. The End-Times Conference 27
Chapter 3. The Signs 41
Chapter 4. The Great Tribulation 66
Chapter 5. The Joy of Being Left Behind 76
Chapter 6. The Real Antichrist 82
Chapter 7. The Rapture Passages 88
Chapter 8. The Kingdom 93
7 Keys to a Healthy Discussion of Scripture 115
Recommended Reading 121
Bibliography 125

FOREWORD

I have known Jordan Hardgrave online through his brilliant humor and insightful perspectives as a teacher. I thoroughly enjoyed his new book, "Jesus Wins". It is a clear, direct explanation of end-time theology without all the malarkey. Although written for the everyman, it isn't simplistic; this is solid, challenging material that you can sink your teeth into. You are going to love it! Or perhaps you will hate it but then love it later when it's truth seeps into your brain. I highly recommend it.

Dr. Jonathan Welton

President of Welton Academy and author of *Raptureless*

February 2018

PREFACE

Let's be honest—prophecy is often very confusing. Somewhere between the ten-horned beast coming out of the sea in the book of Revelation and all the end-time debating, people often discontinue their studies. They ultimately arrive at a view that's jokingly known as, "Pan Millennialism".

This is a way to say, "I don't care anymore, it's all going to pan out in the end anyway. I'm just going to raise my family and worry about the more important aspects of life". I get it—I was in the exact same boat for many years.

To make matters worse, growing up in church I was only presented with one view of prophecy. How was I supposed to decide what to believe about the end-times when I had only heard one perspective? It also didn't help that I wanted to see God's Kingdom come to earth, but had an end-time view that taught a global great tribulation was just on the horizon. Which is it, restoration or evacuation? I never understood what the future looked like and my intuition told me that something was missing. I set out on a journey to find answers that would forever transform my life.

For the first time ever, I could see myself growing old and leaving a legacy. I started to dream about what the world could look like if we partnered with Jesus to see heaven come to earth. What seemed impossible before suddenly appeared possible when I became aware of the Kingdom resources and empowerment available to us through God's Holy Spirit.

In this book, I am going to give you simple tools that anyone can start using today to finally understand Bible prophecy and grasp what the future holds. You will also hear a different view of the end-times that is easily understood and has historical roots that go all the way back to the early church.

In addition, you will discover the many reasons why the end-times are nothing like what we have imagined when we take a closer look at what Jesus said in Matthew 24. The truth is we have every reason in the world to be filled with hope and optimism for the future, and I want to show you from the Scriptures why that is. You have an incredible purpose and assignment on earth, and I want to help eliminate any beliefs that would hinder that truth.

Jesus wants to work with you to transform your city, state, and the nations of the world by advancing His Kingdom and picking up where He left off in His ministry. He promised us that even greater works are available to us now that He has ascended to the Father and sent His Spirit to us, and I believe it's time to see that promise come to pass. God has given you dreams deep within your heart that are worth investing your life in, and I believe a Biblical end-time view is crucial to seeing those dreams come to pass.

Before we can fulfill our Kingdom destiny, we first must be confident we are going to have enough time to fulfill that destiny. Our end-time view shapes our world-view, and our world-view shapes the understanding of our assignment. What I have discovered is that the more hope we have for the future, the more productive we will be in advancing the Kingdom.

I wrote this book because after writing a series of prophecy blogs, the response was overwhelming. Several thousand believers from across the world were writing to me and advising that what I said was redefining everything they believed about the end-times and filling them with hope and understanding. Tears filled my eyes as I humbly realized God was commissioning me to spread an optimistic end-time view with the body of Christ. I don't know about you, but I love being taught from stories, especially true stories. There's something magical about knowing that what you're reading actually happened. There are plenty of books on this subject that list out a set of beliefs and are very long and often difficult to finish. I wanted to write a book on prophecy that read like a thriller novel, yet also included life changing teaching on prophecy and my story of moving from fear to hope. Because this book is a true story, it's best read from cover to cover. I made it short and to the point, so it won't take you more than few hours to finish reading it. I promise that after you read this book, you will never see the end-times the same—ever. What's been a mystery for years is now about to be revealed to you. With more and more "End of the World" predictions coming each year that set the entire globe on edge, now is the time more than ever to take the life changing truth you learn in this book and get out there and spread the good news that Jesus Wins, and the end times are much better than we think. On to chapter one!

CHAPTER 1

The Left-Behind Series

I woke up to what could only be described as my worst nightmare becoming a reality. My heart started pounding as I looked up and observed a darkened church-camp sanctuary filled with hundreds of empty chairs. It happened—I got left behind! I sprang up and ran toward the closest door. Locked! What's happening? I was about ten or eleven at the time, and during the services, I would sit Indian-style and prop my head up so I could doze off. My friends would usually wake me up after service so we could all go eat dinner. This time, nobody woke me up—I was horrified.

Let's go back a second. You may be wondering why I was so afraid of being left behind. I grew up in a small country church in Arkansas, where we were taught the pre-tribulation rapture. You may have heard of it from the popular *Left Behind* books and movies. This belief was fundamental in our church and taught that the righteous on earth would get raptured, while the unrighteous would be left behind. Those that were left would have to endure a global seven-year tribulation period. To some, this was good news, very good news—if they believed, they were righteous. But my wretched soul? Nope. I spent most of my time praying the rapture wouldn't happen in my lifetime. Why? Because I knew I'd be the first one to be left behind. People like me didn't get raptured. Have you ever seen the movie *Problem Child*? That's pretty much who I was, only I don't have red hair.

If I can be honest, this wasn't the first time I had fallen asleep in a church service. Back home, I was the kid snoring under the back row with drool all over my face. At school, I was the class clown that always drove my teachers crazy. I would have all the kids rolling in laughter, but for some reason, my teachers never thought my antics were funny. In first grade, I once got suspended three full days for mooning a kid just because he wouldn't hang out with me at recess. Yes, that really happened. It seems my behavior got worse and worse as I grew up. I made my middle-school band director so upset by being disruptive that he literally kicked me out of the band. Who gets kicked out of middle-school band? It all culminated when my grades were so bad that I failed the eighth grade entirely. I don't remember exactly what my final scores were, but I remember my English teacher calling me over to her desk to inform me that I ended her class with a 4%. Yes, 4%. How is that even possible? She just looked at me for several minutes with utter disappointment, until I finally said, "At least it's not a 3%!" Needless to say, she didn't think it was very funny and sent me directly to detention.

If anyone was going to be left behind, it was me.

Let's go back to me standing in an empty church-camp sanctuary. After going door to door and finding they were all locked, I finally saw a light turn on by the stage. One of the counselors had noticed I was missing from dinner and came to find me. I felt a flood of relief as we walked into the lunch-hall next door, where I saw the other kids safely eating dinner. For me, this kind of thinking all began the moment I watched the first *Left Behind* movie at church in the year 2000.

The End-Times Guy

All the *Left Behind* movies are about what takes place after the rapture. Wait a minute. My church taught the pre-tribulation rapture. That means we believed that as Christians, we would be taken off the earth before the great tribulation. As we watched, I kept wondering why we're spending so much time focusing on a great tribulation we won't even be here for.

Then it hit me. Maybe it's because our parents think that if we don't straighten our lives out—this could be us. Who knows? All I knew is that this movie freaked me out. I'm sure there were some kids there watching who thought, *Awesome, I can't wait for the rapture so I can finally be with Jesus.* Not this guy. The second I saw Kirk Cameron was left behind, I thought, *Yup, that's me. That it so going to be me.*

But I found out I wasn't alone in identifying with the people who were left behind instead of raptured. During the movies, I kept looking around at the other kids, and most of them had this deer-in-the-headlights look on their faces. This was no *Veggie Tales*. All I wanted to see was that talking tomato again. Where's Bob? Where's Larry the Cucumber? Somebody find that cute little cauliflower that encourages us to love Jesus and read the Bible. What's going on? We used to watch the *David and Goliath* VHS tape in children's church and got told we were giant-slayers. Now this? They advertised it as a movie night, and they even had popcorn available. Honestly, I don't see how anyone was able to eat a single kernel. My hands were shaking too much. All I wanted to know after watching this film was "How much time do I have left before I'm left behind, and what's the sign it's about to happen?"

To me, getting left wasn't a matter of if—it was a matter of *when*. When the movie ended, us kids would get into a huddle and ask each other if we would choose to take the mark of the beast and forfeit our soul, or refuse the mark and die of starvation. I always said I would resist the mark and die a martyr, but the problem was I knew myself all too well. I would probably be the first one at the local Antichrist's Grocery & More, scanning my wrist so I could buy a frozen pizza! Once the movies were over, we always had tons of questions. We just had to find some sort of mental clarity that told us we weren't about to experience these frightening events.

There was one man at our church who was the go-to person for all things end-times. Let's call him the End-Times Guy; every church has one. He also happened to reflect the love of God more than anyone I had ever seen. This meant I trusted his words more than anyone else's. He read the Bible constantly and often had monthly teachings for the adults on prophecy. He used one of those huge end-times charts that were a visual representation of how our church believed end-time events would occur. You know, the church gets raptured; then a seven-year tribulation period; then the millennium, or Kingdom Age, etc. I got to sit in on a few of these sessions, and within minutes, something became clear to me. While he was passionate about what he taught, he himself seemed to have more questions than answers.

I remember listening intently to him go back and forth with an older member of our church. This person had raised a question about the tribulation period. There was so much tension in the room you could cut it with a knife. We could all feel the nervousness coming forth in his answers. Sometimes he would say, "For that question, you will have to search the Scriptures on your own time." Or, "That's just a mystery." I knew something wasn't right. When the session was over, I had about ten thousand questions. I decided to find the end-times guy and see if he could give me some answers.

As usual, he lovingly agreed to stop and talk with me. However, as soon as I asked my questions, he just quoted what the pre-tribulation rapture view taught and pointed to the chart. To me, these questions meant everything. I needed to know the fate of my future. If I was going to be left behind, I wanted to know all the details. Where do I buy food? What if I take the mark of the beast? What if I don't take the mark of the beast? It was the end of the world as I knew it, and I wasn't feeling fine. It also didn't help that our church taught that the rapture was going to occur at any minute, which meant I didn't have any time to waste. For all I knew, I was seconds away from entering the darkest hour in human history.

Any Minute Now

I asked Brother Darren if there is anything left to be fulfilled before the rapture. He said, "I don't think so" (12-8-1996).

This quote is from a Bible I have that belonged to someone very close. As you can see, back in 1996, they and someone named Brother Darren believed there wasn't anything that needed to be fulfilled before the rapture occurred. The pre-tribulation rapture view teaches that bad things happening is a sign that this age is ending and the rapture is near. I decided to check and see what types of events happened in America, between 1990 and 1996, which would have led someone to believe the rapture was near. I was shocked to see how similar that time was to today's time:

1990	On July 22, a total solar eclipse occurred.
1991	The Gulf War is waged in the Middle East by a UN-authorized coalition force from thirty-four nations, led by the United States and United Kingdom against Iraq.[1]
1992	Hurricane Andrew, a Category 5 hurricane, kills 65 people and causes $26 billion in damage to Florida and other areas of the US Gulf Coast, and was the costliest natural disaster in history at that time.
1993	The Storm of the Century strikes the Eastern Seaboard, with blizzard conditions and severe weather, killing 300 people and causing $6 billion in damage.

---

[1] Wikipedia, s.v. "Timeline of United States history." Last edited on 13 November 2017, https://en.wikipedia.org/wiki/Timeline_of_United_States_history_(1990–present)

1993   Massive flooding along the Mississippi and Missouri Rivers kill 50 people and devastates the Midwest with $15–$20 billion in damage.

1994   The 1994 Northridge earthquake kills 72 and injures 9,000 in the Los Angeles area and causes $20 billion in damage.

1995   The Oklahoma City bombing kills 168 and wounds 800. The bombing is the worst domestic terrorist incident in US history at the time, and the investigation resulted in the arrests of Timothy McVeigh and Terry Nichols.

1995   A heat wave kills 750 in Chicago, bringing to attention the plight of the urban poor and the elderly in extreme weather conditions.

1995–1996   A budget crisis forces a federal government shutdown for several weeks.

> If bad things happening is the litmus test for a soon-coming rapture, it's no wonder every generation for many years have believed they were the last generation. Bad things happen in every generation.

As you can see, they had many of the events we are seeing today. Wars and rumors of wars, bombings, record-breaking hurricanes, earthquakes, floods, you name it. The truth is, these types of events have happened in every generation to some degree, for a long time. And just like our generation, they have caused many people like me to believe the rapture would occur at any moment. If bad things happening is the litmus test for a soon-coming rapture, it's no wonder every generation for many years have believed they were the last generation. Bad things happen in every generation. After doing a little bit of studying, I found out that many generations have believed the rapture will occur at any moment.

Some of you may remember the booklet that came out in the '80s that included *88 Reasons Why the Rapture Will Be in 1988* and *On Borrowed Time* by Edgar C. Whisenant.[2] He predicted that Jesus was going to rapture the church during the Jewish holiday of Rosh-Hashanah in 1988. Before that day arrived, the World Bible Society, who published this booklet, printed a whopping 3.2 million copies.[3] They even sent 200,000 of them to pastors all across the United States.[4] After his September prediction did not come to pass, Whisenant then decided to make an update and change the prediction to October 3, 1988. Whisenant said, "The evidence is all over the place that it is going to be in a few weeks anyway."[5] Sound familiar?

It's hard to believe I am reading a quotation from 1988, because these days, we are told the exact same thing. Every hurricane, eclipse, blood-moon, earthquake, and war and rumor of war are all said to be prophetic signs—that we are nearing the end. That's why it's important for us to see that this type of end-time speculation has been going on for a very long time. Even with these predictions not coming to pass, Whisenant still kept releasing prediction books entitled *89 Reasons the Rapture Will Occur in 1989*,[6] and additional books predicting 1993[7] and 1994.[8]

And who can forget the buzz that was created with the Y2K scare? I remember in 1999 they had a puppet show at church-camp for us kids, where the puppets with weird voices would say, "In the year 2000," followed by a list of catastrophic events like

"All your computers will shut down!"

"Your cars will stop working!"

[2.] Edgar Whisenant, *88 Reasons Why the Rapture Will Be in 1988/On Borrowed Time*, (Nashville: World Bible Society, 1988).

[3.] "Rapture Seer Hedges on Last Guess," Christianity Today, 21 October 1988, 43.

[4.] "Still Around," Colorado Springs Gazette Telegraph, 14 Sept. 1988, Part D.

[5.] "Rapture Seer," 43.

[6.] Edgar C. Whisenant, Edgar C. (1989). *The Final Shout: Rapture Report 1989* (Nashville: World Bible Society, 1989)

[7.] Edgar C. Whisenant, *23 Reasons Why a Pre-Tribulation Rapture Looks Like It Will Occur on Rosh-Hashanah* 1993 (Little Rock, the Author, 1993)

[8.] Edgar C. Whisenant, (1994). *And Now the Earth's Destruction by Fire, Nuclear Bomb Fire* (Little Rock: the Author, 1994)

"Your phones won't have a dial tone!"

I'm pretty sure they were just trying to be funny during all the end-time speculation, but I remember that I wasn't laughing.

The entire bus ride home, I looked out the window in sorrow. I prepared my heart for the great tribulation period that seemed to be just on the horizon.

I remember lying in bed on New Year's Eve 1999 at about 11:00 p.m. I was tossing and turning all night, praying to God that I lived to see the morning. I was covered in sweat, and my heart was beating so hard I could hear it in my head. I looked over at the clock, and each minute felt like an eternity. I just lay there and looked up at the ceiling, apologizing to God for the life I had lived. Finally, midnight hit. I closed my eyes tightly, clinched my fists, and waited for something big to happen. Nothing.

The sound of silence was piercing my ears. What's the deal? I thought this was supposed to be the end, or the rapture, or something? Just to be safe, I waited until one o'clock to go to sleep. As you guessed, I woke up the next morning still in my sweat-covered bed. This sort of thinking continued as I progressed into my teen years. It wasn't long before my mom and my stepdad also jumped on the end-time bandwagon and started looking for the signs of the end with me.

My mom also grew up being taught the pre-tribulation rapture. In fact, she once went to a church that taught this view constantly for over fifteen years. In high school, we would always watch Glenn Beck on television. Glenn assured us that something terrible and catastrophic was about to happen in the earth. This perfectly confirmed our end-time view. We made sure to watch every single episode to ensure we didn't miss any important details about preparing. Now that we were aware prophecy was being fulfilled all around us, there was always a thick tension in our house. You could say we were rapture-ready. High school graduation was approaching, and the future felt fuzzy. I often wondered why God would allow me to live in such an awful time. I wanted to bring change in the world so badly, but I never thought I would be here long enough. Then, out of nowhere, a light began to shine from a very unexpected person that gave me a glimmer of hope.

The Mysterious Statement That Changed Everything

I'll never forget the moment I glanced over at the TV and saw the strangest-looking preacher I had ever seen. But let me tell you how I got there. One Sunday, I saw new youth pastors walk into the church. I'll never forget it. It was like a stampede of youth and young adults had flooded the sanctuary. They not only had several kids of their own, but they had also taken in foreign exchange students and other youth who were trying to find a purpose in life. These people loved Jesus more than anyone I had ever seen. During the worship services, every single person in their ministry was on their face and crying out to God. One day after service, they invited me to come live at their ministry so I could encounter God too. I moved in, and within weeks, I was back on fire for the Lord and ready to change the world.

They would often have conferences playing on the living room television from various churches. One of the evangelists we watched was named Damon Thompson. I was honestly shocked at who I was looking at. I was used to seeing a clean-cut evangelist that wore suits, ties, and shiny shoes. Damon looked like he just escaped from prison, and often joked that people often said that about him. He had a thick black beard, full tattoo sleeve, and wore blue jeans and a cross necklace when he preached. He also had a deep, raspy voice of authority that made you sit straight up in your seat. Damon had one main message: the Kingdom.

To me, the only thing in my future was the great tribulation. Yet here Damon was, saying God wanted to use me and other believers to rule and reign with Christ to make earth like heaven right now. My intuition was telling me there was truth to what he was presenting. Slowly but surely, my worldview started to shift. I started to entertain the idea that maybe God had something for me to do on this planet besides getting left behind. The problem was, I couldn't shake off this constant sense that maybe Damon was missing it somehow. He kept saying the world was going to get better and better until Jesus comes, which was the opposite of what I was taught about the end-times. I started to hunger for answers as to why he was so optimistic about the future, when clearly the world was as bad as it had ever been. He never devoted a full sermon to talk about the end-times, but every now and then, he would make these mysterious statements that drove me crazy as to what they meant.

One time he stopped in the middle of a sermon and said, "You guys do realize it's the good guys that get left behind, right?"

> You guys do realize it's the good guys that get left behind, right?

Come again? Um, no? Us bad guys get left behind in the rapture, not the good guys. What was he talking about? Hadn't he seen the *Left Behind* series? Maybe he just misspoke. But wait—what if he didn't misspeak? I sat in wonder as I considered the implications of what he was saying. If the good guys were left behind, then what happens to the bad guys? I wanted to give him a chance to explain this clear contradiction, but that moment never came.

Right after saying that statement he said, "That's for another message," and then went on with his sermon. After that, I kept my ears wide open to listen for anything Damon said to bring clarity about the future. I downloaded every single sermon he had ever put on a podcast and listened to them intently, trying to find out what he was talking about. Nothing. The statements were few, and I had more questions than ever. I gave up. He was the only person I had ever heard say the good guys get left behind, or that the world would get better and better until Jesus returns. Who was I supposed to ask about this? I decided to put my end-time view on the backburner and wait for that magical day when I would get answers. Over five years went by. Then, against all odds, something miraculous happened.

CHAPTER 2

The End-Times Conference

It was 2013. My wife and I set sail for Kansas City, Missouri, to be a part of an incredible group of believers called World Revival Church. They often had special speakers flown in from around the world for conferences that covered various topics. At one revival service, we were handed a brochure that advertised "The End-Times Conference," and it stated the following:

> Conference topics include:
>
> Timing the End-Times
> Interpreting Bible Prophecy
> Clearing Confusing Theologies about a Pre-Millennial Rapture
> Ending Victorious!

My mouth dropped to the floor. This had to be the view Damon was talking about. How did I know? I didn't. The only thing I knew was that Damon preached about the church being victorious, and that's exactly what this conference promised to talk about. I immediately looked at my wife and said, "We have to be at this conference." In an instant, all the momentum to understand the end-times came whirling back inside me.

We sat at our table and watched as a man I had never heard of, named Gary DeMar, approached the stage. I sat straight up in my chair because I wasn't going to miss anything. It turns out that Gary had written several influential books about the end-times that were sitting on a table in the front. This guy clearly knew his stuff, and I couldn't wait to hear a full presentation on a different end-time view. I had been waiting for this moment my entire life.

Gary started off by saying, "We have to make a biblical case for whatever we believe about the end-times. If we can't make a biblical case, we have to move on to something else."

> We have to make a biblical case for whatever we believe about the end-times. If we can't make a biblical case, we have to move on to something else.

I remember sitting there thinking, *Nope, can't do it.*

Then Gary did something I didn't expect. Instead of spending several hours talking about beasts with ten horns and the four horses of the apocalypse, he asked us to open our Bibles to Matthew 24.

Why that chapter? I thought all the end-time stuff was in Revelation?

I pulled out my phone and scrolled over to Matthew 24:1.

Then Gary said that Matthew 24 was the clearest chapter on prophecy in the New Testament and was the best place to start studying, not Revelation, which is a book that's often unclear. He also said the reason we don't understand Matthew 24, also known as "the Olivet Discourse," is we do what I did, which is to start at verse 1. The context begins all the way back, in Matthew chapter 21, and this context radically shapes the way we read Matthew 24.

We were also introduced to a principle I had never once heard of growing up in church: audience relevance. Audience relevance is where we consider what a passage meant to the original audience. He also said that the Bible is the best interpreter of the Bible. If we don't understand a passage, all we have to do is turn to other parts of Scripture where the same type of language is used for clarity. It seemed simple enough.

The Parable of the Two Sons
(Matt. 21:28–32)

In this parable, one son tells his father that he won't go to work, but he ends up working anyway. The other son says he will go to work, but ends up skipping work. Jesus asks the religious leaders, "Which of the two sons did the will of his father?"

Of course, the religious leaders say, "The first son."

Jesus then compares the unbelieving chief priest and the elders to the second son who said they would work, but didn't work. In other words, they were all talk and no show.

Well, this seemed to be speaking about the religious leaders, I couldn't deny it.

The Parable of the Vineyard Owner
(Matt. 21:33–41)

Jesus then speaks of a vineyard owner who leased his vineyard to vine dressers whose job is to prune and cultivate the vines, so they are ready to harvest. After that, the vineyard owner goes away to a far country. At harvest time, the vineyard owner sent his servants to gather his share of the harvest. The vine dressers were brutal and beat a servant, killed one, and stoned the other. Despite his servants being murdered, he decided to give it another shot and sent more servants. Sadly, the same thing happened again.

Even though I knew nothing about this parable, I could already sense it was probably speaking about the prophets God had sent to preach repentance, only for them to be beaten and killed. The vineyard owner had so much compassion for the vine dressers that he tried one last time to reach them. This time, he went all out—he sent his own son. I was no prophecy expert, but I knew who this was talking about—Jesus. In the mind of the vineyard owner, surely, they would respect His Beloved Son. Sadly, they killed the son too.

Jesus asked the religious leaders what should be done to the vine growers once the vineyard owner comes back from the far country. They responded by saying the vineyard owner will "bring those wretches to a wretched end, and will give the vineyard to other vine growers who will give him his share of the harvest."

In other words, judgment would come upon them. I looked around the room, and everyone had the same look on their faces as I did: shock. Once again, this seemed to be speaking about the religious leaders.

Then Gary dropped a bombshell.

> When the chief priests and the Pharisees heard Jesus' parables, *they knew he was talking about them*. (Matt. 21:45; italics added)

You could feel everyone at the conference sit a little higher in their chairs as we all realized what we were reading. Wait a minute, if the chief priest and the Pharisees knew these parables were about them, what else was about them? My curiosity was at an all-time high.

The Parable of the Wedding Feast
(Matt. 22:1–14)

A king sent out servants with wedding invites for his son. However, the ones who were invited refused to come.

The king then tries a second time by sending out more servants with invitations. Once again, they refused to come. This time, not only did they refuse the invitation, they also killed the servants who were inviting them.

The king was not happy; in fact, he was furious.

> But when the King heard about it, he was furious. And he sent out his armies, destroyed those murderers, and burned up their city. (Matt. 22:7, NASB)

Gary asked us if we knew what this statement was referring to. I had absolutely no idea. He said Jesus is referring to the Roman destruction of Jerusalem in AD 70, and that nobody from any end-time view disputes that.

The Roman Destruction of Jerusalem and the Temple in AD 66–70

Josephus, a historical scholar, was alive during the Roman destruction of Jerusalem and wrote down exactly what happened. Between AD 66 and AD 70, the Middle East was in revolt against the Romans. It was in AD 69, that Emperor Vespasian left his son Titus to clean up the issues in Judea. In AD 70, General Titus laid siege to Jerusalem, ultimately leveling the temple and burning all of Jerusalem to the ground. In the end, over one million people were killed, many with crosses. It was truly a catastrophe.[1]

At this point, I was turning to my wife every few minutes and saying, "How did we miss this?" Then we read the famous "eight

---

[1] Flavius Josephus, *The Wars of the Jews in The Works of Flavius Josephus, Book V*, William Whiston, Translator, 1734. Accessed November 15, 2017, http://www.sacred-texts.com/jud/josephus/war-5.htm

woes." Now Jesus takes off the gloves and lets the religious leaders have it.

The Eight Woes
(Matt. 23:13–35)

Jesus calls the religious leaders hypocrites six times. He also calls them blind men, blind guides, snakes, and murderers. Jesus goes even further by saying that although they claimed they were not hostile like their fathers, it wasn't true. They had just killed someone named Zechariah between the temple and the altar, showing that they were no different than their fathers. To make matters worse, Jesus says He would send them more prophets and they would also kill them as well. The intended audience in His parables was now fully coming to light—them.

Jesus also says all the righteous blood that had been shed on earth would be poured out on that generation. Notice in the parable of the vineyard owner that the vine dressers were not brought to a wretched end until the vineyard owner had sent several servants, and even his son.

Also, in the parable of the wedding feast, the armies were not sent to destroy the city until those who were invited rejected the invites repeatedly and killed the messengers. It fit perfectly with God sending prophets repeatedly over hundreds of years but people refusing to repent. Then God sent His Beloved Son, and He would end up getting killed too. God didn't want to bring judgment. He never does. It's just that after they reject His Son, what else can He do? If people reject the gift of forgiveness and eternal life, the only thing left is judgment. God was in Christ, reconciling the world to Himself and not counting people's sins against them (2 Cor. 5:19). If people are intent on getting what they deserve, it's their choice, even though it breaks the Father's heart. We see this compassion toward people when Jesus compares Himself to a hen who had been trying to gather her chicks under her wings, but sadly, they were unwilling.

> *If people are intent on getting what they deserve, it's their choice, even though it breaks the Father's heart.*

> Jerusalem, Jerusalem, you who kill the prophets and stone those sent to you, how often I have longed to gather your children together, as a hen gathers her chicks under her wings, and *you were not willing*. (Matt. 23:37; italics added)

Everyone at the conference was now gripped by what we had just read. How could this be? As if I wasn't shocked enough, Gary then read the most shocking end-time statements in existence. No, really, these statements change everything! Of course, I had never heard them a single time in church, and understandably so. Once you hear these statements, you won't ever see the end-times in the same way. I was now determined. For the first time in my Christian life, I had tools to discover what the Bible said about something. This was so unreal. I wasn't looking to a podcast, a video, a sermon, or a book anymore. The power was now in my own hands to discover truth, and I was so excited for the journey ahead.

On the drive home, I just had to tell my beloved mom about what we had heard. I figured she would be very excited to consider other viewpoints about the end-times. I couldn't have been more wrong.

The Consequences of Questioning the Sacred

Have you ever heard of a sacred cow? A sacred cow is a respected belief system that you just don't question. It's a belief system that if you try to mess with it, the cow will start mooing very loudly, and you may even get trampled. Somewhere in the excitement of the conference, I had forgotten just how sacred this belief was to many of the people I love. I had been searching for end-time truth for years, but that didn't automatically mean everyone else was too. Things are about to get messy, so I hope you're sitting down. The conversation with my mom went something like this:

"Hey, Mom. How are you?"

"I am doing great, Jordan. Steve and I are just watching a movie. How's Kansas City?"

"It's been great. We are driving home from a conference about the end-times. I learned so much."

"What did they talk about?"

"Well, this conference has caused me to start asking some questions about the tribulation, the future, and a lot of things."

"What kind of questions? I don't understand."

"I just think we need to at least consider what some passages meant to the original audience."

"Original audience? So you're saying the Bible doesn't apply to us? I'm so confused."

"I'm not saying that at all. I'm just saying the Bible was written for us, but it wasn't written to us. The Bible is full of relevant application directly for you and me today, but when it comes to prophecy, I am learning we need to consider what it meant to those who first heard it. We went through Matthew 21 to 24 using audience relevance, and, Mom, you won't believe what happened. I am so excited to share everything with you. Can you get a Bible really quick?"

> The Bible was written for us, but it wasn't written to us.

"Wait, let me get this straight. You went to a conference and now you're questioning everything you were taught? Aren't you jumping to conclusions? What's wrong with what you believe now?"

"I've been asking questions for a while. I guess I'm just seeing how much I don't know about what the Bible teaches in this subject."

"What? I think you need to give it a few weeks. I get that you're excited, but it will probably wear off."

"But Jesus made some very shocking statements that I heard at the conference. I didn't even know they were in the Bible. Want to hear them?"

"No. I need to get off the phone."

"Wait, I'm sorry. Maybe I came off too strong. I am just starting to have my doubts about what I was taught in church. They said at the conference that the pre-tribulation rapture wasn't really taught until the early 1800s. Do you think they were right?"

"They were wrong. It's always been taught. You can study all you want, and you'll see so."

"Well, anyway, I never meant to upset you. I love you. While I am studying about this stuff, do you think you would at least consider looking into the history of the pre-tribulation rapture while I do as well?"

"I guess, but probably not. I should go lie down. I love you. Bye."

"Bye, Mom. I love you too."

Great. That went absolutely terrible. I had this giant knot in my stomach and felt like I was waging a war against someone's sacred view when I didn't even know what I believed yet. I looked over at my wife and gave her a sad look. She had heard the whole conversation as we were driving and comforted me by saying, "Not everyone is ready to question the view they have held their whole life. Just give it time."

I was ready to throw in the towel again. I wanted answers, but not at the expense of my relationship with my mom. I went home and didn't read the Bible for weeks. I did check the history of the pre-tribulation rapture online to make sure what I told her was correct, but that's it. She didn't call me for over a month.

The Phone Call I Never Expected

"Jordan?" she said.

"Hey, Mom, it's so good to hear from you. I was worried to death we wouldn't speak again. How are you?"

"Good. I decided to research pre-tribulation rapture, like you said."

"What? Are you serious? What did you find?"

"Jordan. I don't know how to say this."

"What? Tell me."

"I still believe in the pre-tribulation rapture, but you were right, it's a newer belief. I can't believe it. I have spent the last month searching every website and book I could find trying to show how people believed this from the start and found nothing. I've been so embarrassed that I have avoided talking to you. From what I read, the pre-tribulation rapture is known as dispensationalism and did not come around until the 1800s with a guy named Darby. John Darby, or something, formulated it. I am just shocked, Jordan. I didn't expect this."

"I know exactly how you feel, and I also have tons of questions. I did some more research on the history of dispensationalism. I also found out that the pre-tribulation rapture view did come on the scene with John Darby in the early 1800s, but it wasn't even well known in the church until the 1909 Scofield reference Bible was released."

"Really? I think I have heard about that Bible before. I want to say my old pastor used to quote from its commentary."

"He probably did, Mom. I saw one in our local Christian bookstore the other day. The Scofield Reference Bible was one of the first of its kind to have a built-in Bible commentary. Back then, this was a huge breakthrough in biblical studies and made the average Christian feel like a scholar. The Scofield Bible was wildly successful and reached the masses. C. I. Scofield took the end-time views of John Darby and put them in the commentary section of this Bible.[2] Shortly after this Bible was published, World War I, the Great Depression, and World War II hit. This was a very unstable time already, but then add in that people were looking in the commentary section of Matthew 24, which read this passage was full of 'warnings, applicable to this

---

[2] For a thorough history of Dispensationalism, read "Who's Right It Is" by Kelley Varner. (Shippensburg: Destiny Image Incorporated, 1996)

present age over which these events are even impending.'³ Suddenly wars and rumors of wars and other things they were seeing were no longer just bad events happening—they were perceived as prophetic fulfillments that were signaling the end of time. This created a pattern which is that now every generation since then looks to Matthew 24 as a prophetic set of signs applicable to them. The cycle repeats itself, and I think we may have just got caught up in the cycle as well. What do you think?"

"I don't know, Jordan. The history is interesting, but what about all those Bible verses that talk about the rapture? I mean, it's everywhere in Scripture."

"I have been waiting to study this out until I knew you and I were at a good place. I don't know anything besides what they said at the conference. Why don't we go on this journey together? Ask me a question, and then let's both study about it and see what we find. Sound good?"

"Okay, sure. I won't be easy to convince, though. Are you sure you're up for the challenge?"

"Hopefully, the Bible will do all the convincing. I am just curious to find out the truth about the end-times. What are you most curious about?"

"How about 1 Thessalonians 4:13–18 and 1 Corinthians 15:51–52. Those are huge verses about the rapture, they must be. Any ideas?"

"I'll be honest, I don't know. But let me study it and we will come back to it later. How about we start with Matthew 24?"

"Why?"

"It's a very clear passage of Scripture that also has multiple parallel accounts from Mark and Luke so we can know exactly what it means.

"Okay sure, Jordan"

"I can't wait. Oh, one thing. When we are reading these passages, let's always consider what they meant to the original audience.

---

3. C.I. Scofield, Reference Notes (1917 Edition), Accessed November 15, 2017. https://www.biblestudytools.com/commentaries/scofield-reference-notes/matthew/matthew-24.html

Also, when we don't understand what a passage means in one place, let's look in other passages of Scripture where the same type of language is used and let the Bible interpret the Bible. I will answer some questions the best I can, but I need your help as well, and now you have the tools to do so. Okay?"

"I guess, but I doubt we'll find anything."

My mom was incredibly skeptical of everything I was saying, but I walked my mom through Matthew 21–23 and showed her the context was speaking to the original audience. She agreed. But she still had tons of other questions. What proceeded after that were weekly conversations about Matthew 24 and other end-time topics that went on for several months. Neither one of us could have prepared for just how amazing the journey ahead would be.

CHAPTER 3

The Signs

The Disciples' Question

> Jesus left the temple and was walking away when his disciples came up to him to call his attention to its buildings.[2] "Do you see all these things?" he asked. "Truly I tell you, not one stone here will be left on another; every one will be thrown down." (Matt 24:1–2)

"Mom, I found out that everyone from all end-time views agree that Jesus is speaking of the destruction of the temple that would take place in AD 70 by the Romans. It's the disciples' question that brings the real controversy."

"I wonder why?"

"Let's read it."

> As Jesus was sitting on the Mount of Olives, the disciples came to him privately. "Tell us," they said, "when will this happen, and what will be the sign of your coming and of the end of the age?" (Matt. 24:3)

"Everyone also agrees that when the disciples asked, 'When will this happen?' they were referring to the destruction of the temple, since Jesus had just said it would be destroyed. It's the last two statements from the disciples about 'the sign of your coming' and 'the end of the age' where there is division. First off, Mark and Luke's account of this verse do not mention 'the sign of His coming' and 'the end of the age.' They just mention 'when will these things happen,' which I think is very interesting."

> Tell us, when will *these things* happen? And what will be the sign that they are all about to be fulfilled? (Mark 13:4; italics added)

> "Teacher," they asked, "when will *these things* happen? And what will be the sign that they are about to take place?" (Luke 21:7; italics added)

"Mom, do you think it's possible that Mark and Luke considered the destruction of the temple, the sign of His coming, and the end of the age as a single event? Maybe that's why they only mention the destruction of the temple and leave out the other details, because the disciples were only asking one question related to the destruction of the temple, but Matthew just chose to give further details as to the implications of the destruction of the temple in his gospel."

"I doubt it, but I guess it's possible. To me, "the sign of Your coming" has to be referring to the final return of Jesus."

"I believe in the final return of Jesus, Mom, but I considered what this statement would have meant to the original audience, and it may be speaking of a judgment coming."

"A judgment coming? What's that, Jordan?"

"I learned that in the Old Testament God "came" in judgment all the time but never appeared physically. After reading Matthew 21–23, it seems the focus is about the destruction of the temple and judgment coming upon the religious leaders of the Old Covenant. I don't think the final return of Jesus would have been on the disciples' minds at this point, especially since they didn't even know He was going to leave yet [John 14:5]."

The Days of Noah

(Matt. 24:38–39)

Jesus compared this judgment coming to the days of Noah. Let me ask you a very important question, Mom. In what way did God allow judgment to be carried out on the wicked people of the world in Noah's time?"

"A flood."

"Correct, and did God ever appear bodily?"

"No, the flood did the job".

"Maybe Jesus is just referring to a coming in judgment that wouldn't involve Him coming bodily."

"I don't know about that, it seems weird. I would have to see a few more examples."

"Jesus did give us another example by comparing this judgment coming to the days of Lot when Sodom and Gomorrah were destroyed.

The Days of Lot
(Luke 17:29–30)

"When Sodom and Gomorrah were destroyed, did God ever show up visibly?"

"No, He didn't. He just allowed fire and brimstone to destroy those cities. Ah, I am starting to see what you mean. But I don't get it. If this is not talking about Jesus showing up physically to bring judgment, how else would He do it?"

"How about an army."

"What do you mean, Jordan?"

"Remember the parable of the vineyard owner where Jesus said "He sent out his armies, destroyed those murderers, and burned up their city? [Matt. 24:7]. The judgment for rejecting the vineyard owner's servants and son was that they, and their city, would be destroyed by armies. Maybe that's why Mark and Luke only mentioned the destruction of the temple, because they knew the temple's destruction was also God coming in judgment upon it. Who else but God would allow the destruction of such a holy place?"

"I guess it's possible, Jordan. It just seems odd that God would use an army to carry out judgment. I don't deny that's what Jesus said would happen in the parable of the vineyard owner. It just seems strange."

"I thought so as well. At first, I couldn't wrap my mind about it, until I looked in the Old Testament. God allowed the Assyrians to carry out judgment on Egypt [Isa. 10:5, 10:6]. God also allowed the Medes to carry out judgment and destroy Babylon [Isa. 13:2–5, 17]."

"Really? I'm going to have to look up those verses. Maybe there is some truth to this. But what about the end of the age? My Bible says the end of the world, which is definitely speaking about the end of everything, or is it?"

"That's a really good question. I have no idea. Let me do a little research and I'll call you back."

"Okay. Talk soon, Jordan."

The End of the Age
(Matt. 24:3)

"Mom?"

"Hey, Jordan. What did you find?"

"It turns out that the Greek word for age here is *Aion*, which usually just means 'a time period.' The Greek word for universe is *Kosmos*, and that Greek word is not used here. Let's remember the following when considering the meaning of 'the end of the age.'"

I then proceeded to remind her about what Jesus said in Matthew 21–24:2:

- The parable of the two sons, vineyard owner, wedding feast, and "eight woes'" were all directed at the religious leaders living in the first century. Even they acknowledged it (Matt. 21:45).
- All the righteous blood that had been shed on earth would be poured out on that first-century group of religious leaders. Unlike previous generations who had crucified prophets, they would be the generation to crucify God's Beloved Son, leaving God no choice but to allow judgment, even though this would break His heart. (Matt. 23:29–35).
- This judgment would be poured out within one generation (Matt. 23:36).
- The temple would be left desolate (Matt. 23:38).
- The temple would be taken down one stone upon another (Matt. 24:2).

> What if the disciples heard Jesus say the temple and religious leaders would be destroyed and knew it meant the end of the Old Covenant age?

"The disciples heard this and concluded that a certain time-period was about to end. Which time-period do you think is represented by the old covenant religious leaders and the old covenant temple?" I asked her.

"I don't know. Your guess is as good as mine."

"The temple was needed for animal sacrifices and for the atonement of sin under the Old Covenant. The religious leaders were needed to carry out the day-to-day aspects of the Old Covenant. What if the disciples heard Jesus say the temple and religious leaders would be destroyed and knew it meant the end of the Old Covenant age? Without a temple and religious leaders, the Old Covenant would be unable to function. Could you imagine the United States government functioning without the president, the secret service, and the White House? In fact, one-third of the Old Covenant laws required a standing temple."

"That would make sense, Jordan. Jesus did not really say anything about the end of the universe while He was in the temple, that's true. But I thought the Old Covenant age ended at the cross when Jesus died and made a New Covenant? What does the destruction of the temple have to do with anything?"

The Great Covenant Transition

I told her, "I agree mom, the old covenant did end at the cross, but it only ended spiritually, not physically. For forty years, the temple was still standing in Jerusalem, and some continued in animal sacrifices. This verse gives us the best picture of what was happening: 'When God speaks of a "new" covenant, it means he has made the first one obsolete. It is now out of date and will soon disappear' [Heb. 8:13, NLT].

"This verse is saying that although the Old Covenant had already become obsolete at the arrival of the New Covenant, it was still yet to fully disappear. How is that possible? Because the Old Covenant did not physically pass away until AD 70, when Jerusalem and the temple were destroyed, ending Old Covenant animal sacrifices for atonement once and for all. The best way to describe this covenant transition is like when you walk outside early in the morning and see the sun coming up but the moon is still visible. The higher the sun goes, the less visible the moon is. Eventually, you can't see the moon anymore."

"Jordan, why did God not destroy the temple immediately after Jesus died? That's what I would have done. Why keep it around for so many years when He was not honoring those animal sacrifices anymore?"

"Good question. The New Testament was written during a very unique transition period where people were leaving the Old Covenant, and entering the new and better covenant. It wouldn't have been fair for God to immediately destroy Jerusalem and the temple without giving enough time for the gospel to go forth so people could decide which covenant they wanted to embrace. Many were offering animal sacrifices because they had not yet heard the gospel preached to them."

"Well, this has given me a lot to think about, Jordan, but I still am very interested to talk about the rest of Matthew 24. Didn't you say there were some shocking statements from Jesus you had to tell me? I'm sorry I didn't want to hear them before. Now I am very curious!"

"Yes, I am going to share them with you soon, but before I do, let's at least look at some of the signs in Matthew 24. You think the statements are shocking? Wait until you see who gets left behind."

"Wait? I have to know. Right now!"

"We will talk about it a little later, Mom. Which sign in Matthew 24 do you want to look at first?"

"Let's start with wars and rumors of wars. That's clearly for our day. Look at the instability in the Middle East, and threats from North Korea of a nuclear world war."

"You may be right. Let me consider it and call you back. I am also going to study the rest of the signs so it may be a few weeks before I call. I really want to know the truth about this stuff too."

"Sounds good. I can't wait."

Wars and Rumors of Wars

"Hey, Mom. How are you?"

"I am doing well. I keep reading Matthew 24 over and over, and I have to tell you, I have found some answers. But most of these verses really have me stumped."

"Well, you will be happy to know that I did find some answers, and they were not what I expected at all. You had mentioned wars and rumors of wars in our last conversation. First off, did you know that when Jesus spoke these words it was during the Pax Romana, which meant 'Roman peace'?"

"Yes! I also found that while I was studying. There weren't any wars going on, so Jesus saying there would be wars at that time would have been a sign to them. Who would have thought?"

"I know, right? I found out that Josephus documented there were so many wars going on at that time that he didn't even need to write about it. He said, 'I have omitted to give an exact account of them, because they are well known by all, and they are described by a great number of Greek and Roman authors.'"[1] Also, there was a Roman historian named Tacitus who lived during this time, and

---

[1]. Flavius Josephus, *The Wars of the Jews, Book IV:9:2*, William Whiston, Translator, 1734. Accessed November 14, 2017. http://www.sacred-texts.com/jud/josephus/war-4.htm

he also documented that there were all kinds of wars going on. He wrote that around AD 70 there were 'disturbances in Germany, commotions in Africa, commotions in Thrace, insurrections in Gaul, intrigues among the Parthians, war in Britain, and war in Armenia.'[2] Just as Jesus said, there were many wars going on in a time of declared peace, which was truly a sign."

"Wow, Jordan, so Jesus really knew His stuff, didn't He? But what about earthquakes increasing? You watch the news. It seems like we are having more and more earthquakes all the time."

Earthquakes in Various Places
(Matt. 24:7)

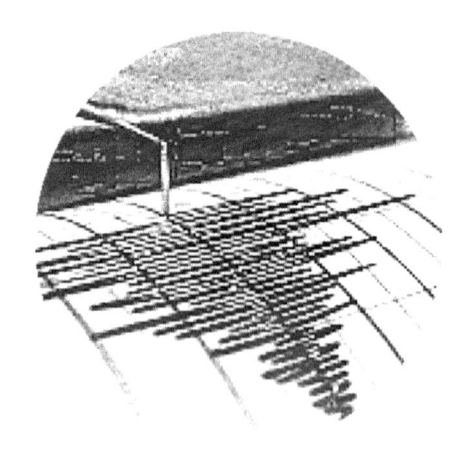

"I thought the same thing, Mom! After I reread the words of Jesus, I found out He never said there would be an increase in earthquakes. He just said there would be earthquakes in various places before the end of the age."

"Really?"

"Yes, I was baffled as well. And there certainly were earthquakes that happened prior to the temple being destroyed. In Matthew 27:51,

---

[2.] Publius Cornelius Tacitus, *History Book 1:2*, Accessed November,15, 2017. http://www.sacred-texts.com/cla/tac/a15000.htm

we read that when Jesus died, 'the veil of the temple was torn in two from top to bottom; and *the earth shook and the rocks were split.*' In verse 54, it says, 'Now the centurion, and those who were with him keeping guard over Jesus, when they saw the *earthquake* and the things that were happening, became very frightened and said, "Truly this was the Son of God!"'"

"Okay, so there was one single earthquake, but that doesn't prove anything. One earthquake is not exactly a sign."

"Wait, there were more. When Mary Magdalene and the other Mary came to see the tomb where Jesus was buried, the Bible says, 'There was a violent *earthquake*, for an angel of the Lord came down from heaven and, going to the tomb, rolled back the stone and sat on it' [Matt. 28:2; emphasis added]. Also, when Paul and Silas were in prison, the Bible says, 'And at midnight Paul and Silas prayed, and sang praises unto God: and the prisoners heard them. And suddenly there was a great *earthquake*, so that the foundations of the prison were shaken: and immediately all the doors were opened, and every one's bands were loosed' [Acts 16:25, 16:26; emphasis added]. Josephus also wrote that one earthquake that happened in Judea was so severe 'that the constitution of the universe was confounded for the destruction of men.'"[3]

"Seriously? Wow. There were earthquakes happening all over the place, weren't there. What about famines? Jesus said there would be famines, and there are famines happening all over the world right now, to my knowledge."

[3.] Quoted in Thomas Scott, *The Holy Bible Containing the Old and New Testaments, According to the Authorized Version, with Explanatory Notes, Practical Observations, and Copious Marginal References*, 3 vols. (New York: Collins and Hannay, 1832), 3:108.

Famines
(Matt. 24:7)

"Remember, Jesus simply said there would be famines before the end of the old covenant age. The only thing needed to prove His words are accurate is to establish there were, in fact, famines in the first century. You may be surprised to find out that the New Testament mentions a famine so severe in Judea that believers as far as Corinth had to send support from other churches [Acts 11:28–30; 1 Cor. 16:1–5; Rom. 15:25–28]. Josephus also wrote about a famine during the Roman siege of Jerusalem that was so severe that the upper rooms of houses were full of women and children who were dying by famine, and the lanes of the city were full of dead bodies."[4]

"That's so sad. I had no idea. Oh, what about 'He who endures till the end shall be saved'? What's that talking about? I always hear it taught that we need to endure to be saved. I thought we were saved by faith in Jesus? This one never made sense to me and still doesn't."

[4.] Flavius Josephus, *The Wars of the Jews, Book V, 12:3*, William Whiston, Translator, 1734. Accessed November 14, 2017. http://www.sacred-texts.com/jud/josephus/war-5.htm.

Endure till the End to be Saved
(Matt. 24:13)

"If someone were to start with Matthew chapter 24, it's very easy to see the word *end* and think it is referring to the end of the world, the universe, or any other end. The question is, which end did the disciples ask about?"

"They asked about the end of the age—well, the end of the old covenant age, right?" She said.

"Yes, that's what I see. All Jesus is saying here is that to make it to the end of the Old Covenant age, which would be marked by all kinds of hurdles, they would need to endure. During this covenantal transition period, there arose a group called Judaizers. These people tried to lure new believers into embracing the law of Moses again. We especially see this happening in Galatians and Hebrews. The believers at the church at Galatia had fallen prey to 'a different gospel' [Gal. 1:8]. It taught them they needed to be physically circumcised to be righteous. These Judaizers were saying that faith was not enough to be born again. The Hebrew believers were so swayed by the Judaizers that they went back to animal sacrifices. Forty years is a long time to wait."

"I thought we had it tough, Jordan. Wow. You would certainly need to endure in that kind of atmosphere. What about being delivered into tribulation? Is that not going to happen to us? I hear about Christians getting martyred all the time."

Delivered to Tribulation
(Matt. 24:9)

"We will always experience tribulation as carriers of light in a dark world, Mom, but it's important to consider audience relevance here. Notice that Jesus says they will deliver *you* up to tribulation, meaning His contemporaries. Just as Jesus predicted, a great persecution arose in the Roman Empire against believers. This persecution included the stoning of Stephen; James, the brother of John, being killed with a sword; Peter being arrested; and John being exiled to the island of Patmos" [Acts 7:59–60, 8:1, 12:1–3; Rev. 1:9].

"Wow, that was truly persecution, who could deny that?" So, let's move on. I have one question that I don't think any one of us can refute. The gospel has not been preached to the entire world yet, there's just no way. There are still people in the jungles of Africa or in distant lands that have never heard the gospel before. I have always believed once the gospel went to the entire globe, then Jesus would return, and that's still what I believe."

The Gospel of the Kingdom Preached to the World
(Matt. 24:14)

"I was taught the exact same thing, but I looked into it and the Greek word for 'world' here is *oikumene*, meaning 'inhabited earth' or 'Roman Empire.' It's the same Greek word used when Caesar taxed the whole world, the Roman world, in Luke 2:1, when Jesus was born. I would imagine Caesar would have liked to tax the entire globe, but he only had authority to tax the Roman Empire, those within his domain. For the physical end of the Old Covenant age to happen, which would be the destruction of the temple, the gospel needed to reach the entire Roman Empire. Remember, God wanted everyone around Judea and Jerusalem to hear the gospel before He allowed the Old Covenant world to be destroyed. So the question is, was the gospel preached to the entire Roman Empire before the destruction of Jerusalem?"

> God wanted everyone around Judea and Jerusalem to hear the gospel before He allowed the Old Covenant world to be destroyed.

"Maybe? I doubt it," she said.

"I couldn't believe it, but the New Testament says it was. Paul said the gospel has come 'in all the world';

'was proclaimed in all creation under heaven'; and 'has been made known to all nations.'" [Col. 1:5–6, 1:23; Rom. 16:25–27].

"Are you serious? Do you know how many people still preach to this day that the gospel has to reach the whole earth before Jesus can return? I would never have guessed Jesus was talking about the Roman Empire and not the globe."

"I am thankful for people wanting the gospel going forth to the whole earth. I want the same thing, Mom. I just don't think that's what Jesus is speaking about in this verse."

"There are some more verses I want you to explain, Jordan. These have me completely stumped."

"Which verses?"

"The first one is when Jesus said, 'Immediately after the distress of those days "the sun will be darkened, and the moon will not give its light; the stars will fall from the sky, and the heavenly bodies will be shaken"' [Matt. 24:29]. There is no way that has already happened."

"At first, I thought the same thing, until I read some passages in the Old Testament that use the same exact language and are not referring to the literal sun, moon, and stars. Maybe it's the same case with this passage. Let's check them out."

"The Stars Will Fall from the Sky"
(Matt. 24:29)

"Mom, do you remember that TV show *Star Search*?"

"Oh yeah, we watched that. It was a talent competition."

"Exactly. It was all about finding the next big star, as in a person with talent."

"So, what's the point, Jordan?"

"The point is, we use these types of metaphors all the time to describe people or things that are not literal stars—so did people in biblical days. The Old Testament often uses stellar language to speak of people. It also uses this language to speak of kings, kingdoms, and nations rising and falling. Remember in Genesis 37:9 when Joseph had a dream and saw the sun, the moon, and eleven stars bow down to him?

"I remember, yes."

"His family interpreted Joseph's dream to mean that *they* would be bowing down to him. They never thought Joseph was referring to the literal sun, moon, and stars bowing down to him. Stars, in particular, are often used in Scripture to speak of all kinds of things that are not literal stars. God told Abraham, "I will surely bless you and make your descendants *as numerous as the stars in the sky* and as the sand on the seashore" [Gen. 22:17; emphasis added]. God told Moses, "The LORD your God has increased your numbers so that today you are *as numerous as the stars in the sky*" [Deut. 1:9; emphasis added]. The Old Testament is also full of examples where the darkening of the sun, the moon, and the stars is referring to the falling of a nation."

"Oh really? Show me an example please."

"Here is a passage that is referring to the destruction of Babylon at the hand of the Medes, yet it uses cosmic language just like in Matthew 24.

> 'See, the day of the Lord is coming—a cruel day, with wrath and fierce anger—to make the land desolate and destroy the sinners within it. *The stars of heaven and their constellations will not show their light. The rising sun will be darkened*

and the moon will not give its light" [Isa. 13:9–10; emphasis added].

"Are you kidding me? That sounds exactly like what Jesus said, almost word for word! This is remarkable, Jordan. So you're saying it was not the literal sun, moon, and stars?"

"I believe so. There is also another example in Ezekiel which speaks about the destruction of Egypt and uses almost identical language to Jesus in Matthew 24:29.

> 'When I snuff you out, *I will cover the heavens and darken their stars; I will cover the sun with a cloud, and the moon will not give its light. All the shining lights in the heavens I will darken over you*; I will bring darkness over your land, declares the Sovereign LORD'" [Ezek. 32:7–8; emphasis added].

"This is so different than what I was taught. I don't know, Jordan. Are we not supposed to interpret the Bible literally? Why should we interpret this passage nonliterally?"

"I think once you hear the shocking statements from Jesus, you will know why we have to interpret this verse nonliterally. Also, don't forget that the New Testament is full of things that shouldn't be taken as literal. Jesus said He was the vine [John 15:5], yet I don't know anyone who believes that Jesus is literally saying He's a plant. Remember when Nicodemus was talking to Jesus and thought Jesus was speaking about literally being born again, as in entering his mother's womb a second time? Jesus was speaking about being born again in the Spirit. Nicodemus missed the understanding because he tried to use a literal interpretation. Also, remember when Jesus said to the Pharisees, 'Destroy this temple and I will raise it again in three days.' He was speaking about the spiritual temple of His body, but they interpreted His words to literally mean that he would destroy the physical temple of Jerusalem and rebuild it in three days which was impossible to do."

"The Son of Man Coming on the Clouds of Heaven"
(Matt. 24:30)

"Jordan, please don't tell me you believe Jesus has already come on the clouds of heaven, there's no way that could have happened. Don't you think everyone would have noticed Jesus up in the clouds riding around in the first century?"

"You're right, and that's why I believe it's important we look at what the Old Testament has to say about the meaning of clouds which is often non-literal. In Isaiah 19:1, the Lord is described as 'riding on a swift cloud' and 'about to come to Egypt.' This language sounds literal, yet is referring to a judgment upon Egypt. Joel 2:1–2 says that when the Lord brings judgment, it's likened to 'a day of clouds and thick darkness.' Zephaniah 1:14–15 says that when the Lord brings judgment, it's considered 'a day of darkness and gloominess, a day of clouds and thick darkness.' Ezekiel 30:3 says that when the Lord comes in judgment, it is 'a day of clouds, a time of doom for the nations.'"

"Also, in regard to the Lord 'coming,' there are plenty of examples in the Old Testament where the Lord 'came' but never appeared visibly. Remember, you and I both believe Jesus will return visibly someday which other passages speak about, but I believe Matthew 24 is speaking about a judgement coming of Christ, not His bodily coming at the end of time. In Genesis 11:5, it says 'the Lord came down to see the city and the tower the people were building,' which is speaking about the construction of the tower of Babylon. We know that while God knew what was happening, He never appeared physically.

"In Exodus 3:8, God said He 'came down' to deliver the Israelites out of Egyptian captivity, yet He never physically came. God also appeared as clouds all through the Old Testament yet never appeared physically (Ex. 13:21; 14:24; 19:9; 20:21; 33:9; 34:5; 1 Kings 8:12]. Mom, maybe this is Jesus speaking about judgment and using Old Testament language they would have been familiar with?"

"It could be possible. I don't know. This one is tough for me. Do you have any other evidence to support a nonliteral interpretation of this verse?"

"I have a couple things to add. Jesus told those witnessing His trial before Caiaphas '*you* will see the Son of Man sitting at the right hand of the Mighty One and coming on the clouds of heaven' indicating *they* would see it [Matt. 26:24; emphasis added]. The church historian Eusebius wrote that when James was asked about the coming of the Son of Man, he responded by saying 'He is now sitting in the heavens, on the right hand of great Power, and is *about* to come on the clouds of heaven.' James was killed for saying that statement around AD 62, which was right before the destruction of Jerusalem in AD 70. It seems James, like everyone in the pre–AD 70 church, was looking for the Lord to come in judgment upon the system that was bringing severe harassment to the New Testament church.[5] Paul told the Thessalonians that when the Lord came in judgment, it would give relief to him and his contemporaries from the persecution they were receiving from the Judaizers [2 Thess. 1:4–10]. This

> This was a coming in judgment they not only expected in their day, but desperately needed.

[5.] Eusebius, *Ecclesiastical History*, Book 2, Chapter XXIII, AD 325. Accessed November 15,2017. http://www.preteristarchive.com/ChurchHistory/0325_eusebius_history.html.

was a coming in judgment they not only expected in their day, but desperately needed."

"I can't deny what you're saying, Jordan, but I am not fully on board yet. Can I ask you a question? Why are you so insistent on a nonliteral interpretation of some of these passages?"

"Okay, I think it's time to reveal the shocking statements of Jesus."

"Finally, Jordan! I have been waiting an eternity."

"The reason I believe the signs in Matthew 24 were for those living in the first century is because of what Jesus says right after He lists the signs.

> 'Truly I tell you, *this generation* will certainly not pass away until *all* these things have happened' [Matt. 24:34; emphasis added].

"In addition, He says earlier,

> 'For the Son of Man is going to come in his Father's glory with his angels, and then he will reward each person according to what they have done. Truly I tell you, *some who are standing here will not taste death before they see the Son of Man coming in his kingdom*' [Matt. 16:27–28; emphasis added].

"He also says, to His disciples,

> 'When you are persecuted in one place, flee to another. Truly I tell you, *you will not finish going through the towns of Israel before the Son of Man comes*' [Matt. 10:23; emphasis added].

These statements place His coming in judgment and the signs leading up to that judgment in the first century, since a generation is usually believed to be about forty years [Num. 32:13] and some of the people standing there would not be alive today, over two thousand years later of course.

"There are passages about the final bodily coming of the Lord we will discuss later, but I believe these verses must be speaking about a nonliteral judgment coming of the Lord due to the timing described."

"You were right, those are shocking! I can't believe what I just heard."

"You're not the only one. Look at what C. S. Lewis had to say about Matthew 24:34 and the time statements of Jesus."

> "The apocalyptic beliefs of the first Christians have been proved to be false. It is clear from the New Testament that they all expected the Second Coming in their own lifetime. And worse still, they had a reason, and one which you will find very embarrassing. Their Master had told them so. He shared, and indeed created, their delusion. He said in so many words, 'This generation shall not pass till all these things be done.' And He was wrong. He clearly knew no more about the end of the world than anyone else. This is certainly the most embarrassing verse in the Bible.[6]

"C. S. Lewis was like most of us. He thought Jesus was saying He would come bodily before that generation passed away, which is known as the Second Coming of Christ, which, of course, won't happen until the end of time. He also thought Jesus was speaking about the end of the planet Earth in Matthew 24, which we have already shown is highly unlikely. I think it's important to point out that even the term "second coming" is problematic to begin with because if we think about it, there are many comings of Jesus in Scripture. The Old Testament is full of judgement comings of the Lord yet we never count those. Jesus was born and came to earth from heaven which could be called His first coming. He died and came back from the grave which could be called His second coming. He came with the

---

[6] C.S. Lewis, *The World's Last Night and Other Essays*, (New York: Harcourt, Brace and Company, 1960), 98.

Holy Spirit on the day of Pentecost which could be called His third coming. He came in judgement on Jerusalem in AD 70 which could be called His fourth coming. And He will come bodily at the end of the time which would make that His fifth coming if we were counting each coming. I think it's best to simply look at each event in its context as the Bible presents them rather than add labels that only cause more confusion. With that being said, even non-Christians have seen the clear time statements of Jesus, and have even used them to conclude that Jesus can't be the Son of God because they believe He prophesied something that didn't happen.

"Listen to what the self-proclaimed atheist, Bertrand Russell, said in his book *Why I Am Not a Christian.*

> 'I am concerned with Christ as He appears in the Gospel narrative as it stands, and there one does find some things that do not seem very wise. For one thing, He certainly thought that His second coming would occur in clouds of glory before the death of all the people who were living at that time. There are a great many texts that prove it. That was the belief of His early followers, and it was the basis of a good deal of His moral teaching.'"[7]

"Once again, Betrand Russell is assuming since the Bible mentions a "coming" of Jesus, that it must be speaking about His "second coming" which is understood to be His final bodily coming at the end of time. Since Jesus did not return bodily before the first century generation passed away, Betrand assumed Jesus was a false prophet and couldn't truly be the Son of God. All he had to do was look in the Old Testament and he would have discovered Jesus doesn't have to show up bodily to bring judgement. I believe Jesus did come in judgment within a generation, before some standing in front of Him died, and before His followers finished going through the cities of

---

[7.] Bertrand Russell, *Why I Am Not a Christian*, (Watts & Co., for the Rationalist Press Association Limited, 1927). Accessed on November 15, 2017, https://users.drew.edu/jlenz/whynot.html.

Israel, just as He said. The reason I can believe Jesus is a true Prophet is because the judgment upon the temple and the religious leaders was carried out through the Roman armies, and Jesus didn't have to return bodily for that to happen."

"I do see what you're saying, Jordan, but how do we know Matthew 24:34 is not speaking about a different generation?"

"There certainly have been many attempts to adjust the words of Jesus here to make a future generation," I said. "I understand why too. If Jesus really meant what He said, it means we should not be looking for any of the signs in Matthew 24 in our generation. Some say Jesus meant 'This Jewish race' will not pass away until all those things take place. The problem with that is Jesus uses the Greek word 'Genea' for generation here, and it doesn't mean race. The Greek word for race is *Genos*, which means 'race, offspring, or countrymen.' *Genea*, the word Jesus does use, refers to a whole multitude of men living at one time—a generation. In Jewish thinking, this spanned forty years, the time it took the wicked, unbelieving generation to perish in the wilderness before the next could possess the promised land [Num. 32:13]. Also, every other time Jesus uses the statement 'This generation,' it always refers to the generation He is speaking to, never a future generation. Others say it's 'the generation that sees all these signs' that will not pass away until all those things take place. The only problem is Jesus said, 'This generation will not pass away until all these things take place' and did not say 'the generation that sees these signs.' In order for that interpretation to work we must change the word 'this' to 'the' and then add 'that sees these signs' after generation, things Jesus never said."

"You've made some great points, but I have one more question about Matthew 24—the great tribulation. We are supposed to be raptured out before it, right?"

"Well, are you sitting down?"

"Oh no, Jordan. What is it?"

"I am sorry to say that everything we were taught about the great tribulation may be contrary to what Scripture teaches."

"Oh my gosh, what is it?"

"Let's talk about it tomorrow when we have more time to discuss it. This one is going to take a little bit to explain."

"You're going to make me wait? I guess I will have to. Okay, talk to you then, Jordan."

CHAPTER 4

The Great Tribulation

(Matt. 24:21)

"Mom?"

"Hey, Jordan. Okay, I am ready to learn about the great tribulation."

> Jesus said they would be able to escape the 'great tribulation' if they followed His exact instructions.

"Awesome, this is going to be a huge eye-opener. Let me start by asking you a question. Did you know Jesus said the great tribulation could be escaped by simply fleeing to the mountains from Judea?"

"Wait, could you say that again?"

"Yes. In fact, Jesus says the great tribulation could be escaped—twice. He first said to pray their 'flight' from the great tribulation would not take place in the winter or on the Sabbath [Matt. 24:20]. The Greek word for flight here is *phyge*, which means 'escape to safety.' Those believers living in the first century were unable to escape the general persecution that arose against them as we have shown. However, Jesus said they would be able to escape the 'great tribulation' if they followed His exact instructions. Even so, certain circumstances may hinder that escape which is why Jesus told them to pray the great tribulation did not occur at certain times or during certain events."

The Winter

"If people were trying to escape during winter, or stormy conditions, it would greatly hinder them. Remember, they would be fleeing by foot or animal, which is difficult enough by itself."

The Sabbath

"Strict travel laws at that time stated that, on the Sabbath, no person could walk more than "a Sabbath day's journey" which was about a quarter-mile (Acts 1:12). The consequences of walking more than a quarter mile would include severe punishment up to being arrested. We also know from Scripture that the city gates to Jerusalem were closed during the Sabbath and guarded by the Levites. This prevented people from bringing loads of food in and out and working when they were supposed to be resting."[1]

"Pregnant Women and Nursing Mothers"
(Matt. 24:19)

"Jordan, I remember when I decided to have you and your brothers. At first, I thought about this verse and wondered if it was even wise to have kids, because I may end up not being able to escape the great tribulation. What is this verse really talking about?"

"Well, Mom, first, I want to say thank you for deciding to have us kids! But as to the Scripture verse, it goes like this: If a

---

[1.] See Nehemiah 13:15, 13:22; Jeremiah 17:21, 17:24.

mother was nursing or caring for a small child, it would slow them down in their attempts to escape the great tribulation. I remember when my wife was pregnant. Her feet became so swollen she could barely walk at times. Plus, carrying our daughter around as a small baby meant we had to be extra careful, since we were now looking out for another life." While being pregnant or nursing would have been a bad idea for people living in Judea just prior to the destruction of Jerusalem, women living now can rest assured this verse doesn't apply to them.

"Let No One in the Field Go Back to Get Their Cloak"
(Matt. 24:18)

"Get ready, Mom, because you're about to find out that the great tribulation is nothing like the way we were taught. Let's look at a few more verses. Jesus said that leaving the field to enter your house and get your cloak would be unsafe. Yet simply not returning from the field to get your cloak would keep you safe. If Jesus was referring to a global tribulation, fleeing to any field on planet earth wouldn't help make you safe."

"Let No One on the Housetop Go Down to Take Anything Out of the House"
(Matt. 24:17)

"Flat roofs are uncommon for us, but in first-century Israel, they were very common. Most houses had flat roofs at that time. It was much cooler on the roof, and roofs were used for sleeping and living quarters, and for entertaining guests.[2] According to Jesus, staying away from your house would keep you safe, while entering in to get something you forgot made you unsafe."

---

[2] See Deuteronomy 22:8; Luke 5:19.

"Then Let Those Who Are in Judea Flee to the Mountains"
(Matt. 24:16)

"Now we get to the second time Jesus stated the great tribulation could be escaped. Remember how we looked at the Greek word *phyge* that Jesus used when He said, 'Pray your *flight* [escape to safety] does not take place in winter or on the Sabbath' [Matt. 24:20]?" This is the same Greek word *phyge*, used here. Jesus is saying that by fleeing to the mountains from Judea, His followers could safely escape the great tribulation."

"I think I see it now, Jordan. The great tribulation can't be global if it could be escaped. But if the great tribulation was not global, where would it take place?"

"I'm glad you asked. By looking at Luke's account of Matthew 24:16, we see where the great tribulation would happen."

> Then those in Judea must flee to the hills. *Those in Jerusalem* must get out, and *those out in the country should not return to the city.* (Luke 21:22; emphasis added, NLT)

"Here's what I am seeing in these passages, Mom. Everything Jesus is saying is directed at getting people out of Jerusalem, once the great tribulation period started. Why? Because Jerusalem is the city where the great tribulation would occur. Jesus loved people so much, that He did not want anyone getting caught up in the tribulation that would occur once the Roman armies invaded Jerusalem and eventually burned it to the ground."

> Jerusalem is the city where the great tribulation would occur.

"This makes so much more sense than what I was taught, Jordan. How did they know when it was time to flee?"

"We know what the sign to flee was by once again looking at what Luke had to say about these events."

> *When you see Jerusalem being surrounded by armies, you will know that its desolation is near.* Then let those who are in Judea flee to the mountains, let those in the city get out, and let those in the country not enter the city. For this is the time of punishment in fulfillment of all that has been written. (Luke 21:20–22; emphasis added)

"Luke says that a sign the followers of Jesus needed to flee to the mountains from Judea would be when *they* see Jerusalem surrounded by armies. The historian Josephus records that in AD 70, the Roman army encompassed Jerusalem under the command of Caesar Titus and then seized and ultimately destroyed the entire city."[3]

"That is very fascinating. The only problem is, I don't think the Bible shows any believers fleeing to the mountains, does it?"

---

[3] Flavius Josephus, *The Wars of the Jews, Book VII*. Chapter 1.1 2, William Whiston, Translator, 1734. Accessed November 14, 2017, William Whiston, Translator, 1734. Accessed November 14, 2017, http://www.sacred-texts.com/jud/josephus/war-7.htm.

Flight to Pella

"Your right, Mom. The Bible doesn't mention the flight to the mountains, because it was written prior to the destruction of Jerusalem. However, Eusebius,[4] Epiphanius,[5] and other church fathers confirm that prior to the destruction of Jerusalem, Christians fled to a town called Pella, which was in the region of Perea. This would have been ample distance from the great tribulation, which would take place in Jerusalem."

"What about all the tribulation that Christians are facing?" She asked. "Are you saying that's not happening? Christians are dying all over the place."

"I don't deny that. I am grieved that all around the world there is currently Christian tribulation and persecution taking place. My heart aches for this situation, and my prayers are with those who

---

[4.] Eusebius, *Ecclesiastical History, Book 3*, Chapter V, AD 325. Accessed November 15, 2017. http://www.preteristarchive.com/ChurchHistory/0325_eusebius_history.html.

[5.] Epiphanius, *Epiphanius' Treatise on Weights and Measures, the Syriac Version*, ed. James Elmer Dean, (Chicago: University of Chicago Press, 1935.)

are carrying the gospel in the darkest places of the earth. I believe the Bible teaches the great tribulation is in the past, but that doesn't mean Christians are not experiencing tribulation in general that is extreme and disheartening, and we should support them in any way we can."

"But Jordan, how do you know we won't also experience the great tribulation? Maybe AD 70 was just a preview of a worse tribulation to come?"

> Jesus said the great tribulation would take place before the generation He was speaking to passed away [Matt 24:34]. Also, He said it would never be repeated [Matt. 24:21].

"Good question. For one, Jesus said the great tribulation would take place before the generation He was speaking to passed away [Matt 24:34]. Also, He said it would never be repeated [Matt. 24:21]. Plus, once we see that Matthew 24 is simply signs leading up to the physical end of the Old Covenant age, the only way for anything in Matthew 24 to be repeated is if God were to allow the temple to be rebuilt, reinstitute animal sacrifices for atonement, then have Jerusalem and the temple destroyed all over again. That was a one-time event that won't ever be repeated because the New Covenant has made the Old Covenant obsolete forever. Also, there is nothing in the context that communicates the great tribulation or anything in Mathew 24 will have a double fulfillment."

"Well, Jordan, this has been quite the revealing day. Didn't you promise me you would also talk about being left behind as well?"

"Absolutely, that is going to be a very fun conversation. The Scriptures are actually crystal clear about who gets left behind, and I'm pretty sure now that it's not who the Left Behind series says it is. We have gone over a lot today, let's chat tomorrow. Also, I just did a little research on the Antichrist, and I know who Antichrist is."

"You do! Who is he?"

"A better question may be 'who were they'. I'll save it for later. Talk to you soon, Mom."

"Seriously? You keep leaving me hanging. I will talk to you later."

CHAPTER 5

The Joy of Being Left Behind

Local television stations from around the world reported bizarre occurrences, especially in time zones where the event had happened during the day or early evening. CNN showed via satellite the video of a groom disappearing while slipping the ring onto his bride's finger. A funeral home in Australia reported that nearly every mourner disappeared from one memorial service, including the corpse; while at another service at the same time, only a few disappeared and the corpse remained. Morgues also reported corpse disappearances. At the burial, three of six pallbearers stumbled and dropped a casket when the other three disappeared. When they picked up the casket, it too was empty."[1] -Left Behind, Page 47-48

"Hey, Mom, are you ready to get left behind?"

---
[1] Tim LaHaye and Jerry B. Jenkins, *Left Behind*, (Carol Stream: Tyndale House, 1995.) 47-48

"What do you mean? No, I am not!"

"You'll understand at the end. I remember when I first heard the statement 'The good guys get left behind.' It was so odd to me since I was taught the good guys got raptured. I decided to look at what the Scriptures teach, and I was baffled to find it's true—the good guys do get left behind. Let's look at the Scripture that is commonly used to describe a rapture event where the righteous are raptured and the unrighteous are left behind:

> 'Two men will be in the field; one will be taken and the other left. Two women will be grinding with a hand mill; one will be taken and the other left'" [Matt. 24:40–41].

"I don't know, Jordan, to me, that sounds like two people are walking through a field and one gets raptured and the other one gets left behind. That's what we were taught growing up at least."

"Remember how we determined that the Scripture teaches the great tribulation could be escaped by simply fleeing to the mountains from Judea, and Jerusalem being surrounded by armies being a sign it was time to flee?"

"Yes, that was a huge shock since I thought the great tribulation was speaking about a worldwide event. I had no idea it could be escaped. I have been telling my friends at work about that."

"I believe the verses about one being left and one being taken are actually referring to two different responses to the great tribulation. When people saw the great tribulation coming upon Jerusalem, they could either choose to remain there and be killed by the Romans, or flee from Jerusalem and be left alive. Let's lay aside any ideas we may have about this and just look at

> *I believe the verses about one being left and one being taken are actually referring to two different responses to the great tribulation.*

what the Scripture teaches for a moment. It's actually pretty clear once we remove the lens of what we were taught."

"Sounds good."

"Alright, Mom, so pretend your house was burning down. Let's say someone you loved was inside and had passed out from smoke inhalation. You had to save them, so you run in and carry them out safely. Once you are out, you remember your Grandma's Bible was still inside. Because of the sentimental value, you decide at the last minute to risk your life and turn back to retrieve it. At that point, it's too late. The firefighters are trying to extinguish the roaring blaze, but you ignore the warning and run in anyway. They are screaming at you, 'This thing is coming down any minute, it's time to flee!' You ignore their instructions and rush inside to grab your Grandma's Bible, only for the roof to collapse and take your life. Similarly, I believe Jesus is telling them that when they see Jerusalem surrounded by armies, it's too late to turn back at that point. And if they turn back, they will be destroyed."

Who Gets Taken?

"Remember, Jesus gives two examples to illustrate what it will be like when one is left and one is taken. He compares that time of tribulation and judgment to 'the days of Noah,' and 'the days of Lot.' Matthew 24:37–39 says, "The flood came and took them all away." Who do you think Jesus is referring to when He says 'them'? Noah, or the ungodly people that had taken over the world?"

"I don't know, Jordan. I have always been taught that Noah's flood represents the rapture taking Noah and his family away."

"In Matthew's version, it's hard to come to any solid conclusions. Thankfully, Luke gives us a more detailed account of the days of Noah and says, "The flood came and destroyed them all" [Luke 17:26, 27].

"Noah and his family were not destroyed by the flood or taken off guard—the rest of the world was. Noah and his family were well prepared for it in advance and built the boat to heed the warning from God that judgment was just on the horizon. It was the rest of the unbelieving world that went on 'marrying, eating, drinking' as if everything was business as usual. I want you to hear these two statements again—Matthew's account and Luke's account of Jesus's words, and it reveals the destiny of the one who is taken.

> "The flood came and *took them all away*."
> "The flood came and *destroyed them all*."

"Wait a minute, so the one being taken is the one who was destroyed? That would mean the one left behind was Noah and his family? That's opposite of what the Left Behind series says! I just can't believe we have been believing it backward. Do you know what this means? Millions of people are believing the opposite of what the Bible says."

"Wait, it gets even clearer. Let's go directly to the flood in Genesis and see who is left behind."

> Every living thing on the face of the earth was wiped out; people and animals and the creatures that move along the ground and the birds were wiped from the earth. *Only Noah was left, and those with him in the ark.* (Gen. 7:23, emphasis added)

"Wait until you hear the second example Jesus gave comparing His judgment coming to 'the days of Lot.' This is where we are really going to see the meaning of "Two men will be in the field; one will be taken and the other left.'

> It was the same in the days of Lot. People were eating and drinking, buying and selling, planting and building. But the day Lot left Sodom, fire and sulfur rained down from heaven and destroyed them all. (Luke 17:28-29)

"In the story of Lot, the people of Sodom and Gomorrah were destroyed by the fire and sulfur that rained down upon them. Lot, who was righteous, was left behind and spared—he didn't get taken anywhere. However, his wife looked back at the destruction and turned into a pillar of salt. This is a perfect illustration of two different responses to the great tribulation. Fleeing led to safety, remaining led to destruction. Jesus even specifically mentions Lot's wife as an example not to follow once they observed the great tribulation coming upon them."

> Fleeing led to safety, remaining led to destruction.

> On that day no one who is on the housetop, with possessions inside, should go down to get them. Likewise, no one in the field should go back for anything. *Remember Lot's wife!* (Luke 17:31–32, emphasis added).

"The original audience knew exactly what Jesus meant by one being left behind and one being taken when He compared it to the days of Noah and then Lot and his wife (Gen. 19:23–26). Jesus is following the same train of thought throughout the entire narrative. He is giving them a warning about the consequences of remaining in Jerusalem when it was about to be destroyed."

"What about the passage where it says two will be in one bed, one will be taken, the other left? That must be talking about a rapture though. How could it not?"

"Let's look at it in light of what we have just learned."

> "I tell you, on that night, two people will be in one bed. One will be taken and the other left" (Luke 17:34).

"I believe Jesus is painting a picture of the different responses of two people who are asleep in Jerusalem on the night it's time to flee. One person will get up from their bed, flee Jerusalem, and head to the mountains. The other will stay comfortably in their bed and remain to be taken captive and ultimately destroyed. Luke even gives us more evidence that the one who is taken is the one being destroyed."

> "Where, Lord?" they asked. He replied, "Where there is *a dead body*, there *the vultures will gather*." (Luke 17:37, emphasis added).

I continued. "Those who remained in Jerusalem would be taken, and their dead bodies would be surrounded by 'vultures,' which is the Greek word *aetos*, which means "eagle." The eagle was the sign of the Roman legion and the symbol of the Roman army's power."[2]

"I have to tell you, I will never believe the same way after what I just heard. This changes everything. Now can we talk about the Antichrist?"

"Sure, I hope you're sitting down . . ."

"Oh no, here we go again."

---

[2] Did Eagles Carry Emperors into Heaven? Accessed November 15, 2017, http://www.bible-history.com/archaeology/rome/2-roman-eagle-bb.html.

CHAPTER 6

The Real Antichrist

"Mom, I believe in antichrist, but I am not so sure the Bible teaches about *the* Antichrist, as in one single guy who will rise up at the end of time. First off, it's important to remember that we are not the first generation to believe that we will soon see the rise of an individual called the Antichrist. I'm going to read a quote to you, and tell me what year you think this was said in: 'There is no doubt that the Antichrist has already been born. Firmly established already in his early years, he will, after reaching maturity, achieve supreme power.'"

"I am going to guess within twenty years ago, because the Antichrist can't be that old."

"Mom, you won't believe it, but I was shocked to find out that this statement was made by Saint Martin of Tours who was born in AD 316 and died in AD 397.[1] I thought the same as you. I thought

---

[1] Richard Abanes, *End-Time Visions*, (New York: Four Walls Eight Windows, 1998).

our generation was the first one to look for *the* Antichrist to rise, but it turns out this is nothing new. Here is another quote, written 1600 years after the first one by Dave Hunt in 1990."

> Somewhere at this very moment on Planet Earth, the Antichrist is almost certainly alive—biding his time, awaiting his cue. Banal sensationalism? Far from it! That likelihood is based upon a sober evaluation of current events in relation to Bible prophecy. Already a mature man, the Antichrist is perhaps active in politics and might even be an admired world leader. Or he could be the head of a multinational corporation, a little-known international banker of great wealth and behind-the-scenes influence, a sports hero—or he might arise suddenly from total anonymity. Somewhere he is being meticulously groomed, though as yet he probably has no more inkling than do those who encounter him daily of the ultimate role for which Satan is preparing him and will, one momentous day, utterly possess him.[2]

"Wow, those quotes sound almost identical."

"It's because there have been several generations that believed they would be the ones to see the Antichrist rise. Joachim of Fiore [1135–1202] predicted the Antichrist would rise around AD 1260.[3]

"So why does every generation think they are the ones who will see this guy rise up?"

"Great question, Mom. I think it's because we may not have looked to the Bible for our definition of *antichrist*, but have looked to the Left Behind series or other prophecy books. They define the Antichrist as one single individual who has incredible power and uses it for evil. That's why people seem to always predict it's the president of some country, who is the Antichrist."

---

[2] Dave Hunt, *Countdown to the Second Coming*, The Berean Call (April 19, 2012).
[3] Abanes, *End-Time Visions*, 399.

"That could be true, but I thought the Antichrist was all over Scripture?"

"First off, you will probably find it shocking to know that the word *Antichrist* is completely absent from the most prophetic book in the entire Bible—Revelation. The same John that wrote the first, second, and third books of John, is the same John that wrote Revelation. You would think John would mention him in Revelation at least once if he were such a critical figure."

> The word Antichrist is completely absent from the most prophetic book in the entire Bible—Revelation.

"Wait, what?" she asked, reluctantly. "You're telling me that the Antichrist is not even mentioned in Revelation one time? That's hard to believe. I will have to look that up. So where is he mentioned then?"

"The word *antichrist* appears just four times in the entire Bible, three times in First John, and one time in Second John. Let's look at each occurrence and see if we can figure out what it's talking about."

> Dear children, this is the last hour; and as you have heard that the antichrist is coming, even now many antichrists have come. This is how we know it is the last hour. (1 John 2:18)

"Notice that John states there were many 'antichrists,' who had already appeared in the first century when this letter was written. These people were an indicator that it was 'the last hour.' This indicates that 'antichrist' are a group of people, not just one single individual. But what are the attributes of these people John calls antichrist? We find out the next time this term is used."

> "Who is the liar? It is whoever denies that Jesus is the Christ. Such a person is the antichrist— denying the Father and the Son. (1 John 2:22)

"John defines 'antichrist' as anyone who denies that Jesus is not the Christ."

> This is how you can recognize the Spirit of God: Every spirit that acknowledges that Jesus Christ has come in the flesh is from God, but every spirit that does not acknowledge Jesus is not from God. This is the spirit of the antichrist, which you have heard is coming and even now is already in the world. (1 John 4:2–3)

"Here's where we really begin to see the identity of Antichrist unfold even further, Mom. In addition to denying that Jesus was the Christ, these people also denied that Jesus came in a physical body. John also reiterates that the spirit of antichrist was already in the world. The final occurrence of the word *antichrist* is this: 'I say this because many deceivers, who do not acknowledge Jesus Christ as coming in the flesh, have gone out into the world. Any such person is the deceiver and the antichrist [2 John 1:7].'

"So far, we know this about antichrist.

1. They are many people, not just one.
2. They were living in the first century.
3. They denied Jesus as being the Christ.
4. They denied that Jesus had a physical body."

"So, who do you think these people were, then?"

"We can't be a hundred percent sure, but after my studies, I believe these people were most likely first-century Gnostics. Gnostics have always been, and remain to this day, a very mysterious group.[4] We only know bits and pieces about what they believed. One of the fundamental beliefs of Gnosticism was that 'all matter is evil.' To a Gnostic, a holy and spiritual God would never wrap Himself in evil human flesh. This is a problem because these Gnostics were deny-

---

[4.] The Gnostic World View: A Brief Summary of Gnosticism, The Gnosis Archive. Accessed on November 12, 2017, http://gnosis.org/gnintro.htm.

ing the incarnation, the glorious moment we celebrate as Christians when, 'the word became flesh and dwelt among us' [John 1:24], which is the essence of the gospel itself. If Jesus did not have a physical body, that would necessitate that His blood was not shed, which means our sins are not forgiven. John knew how poisonous this belief was to the church. Because this denial was so contrary to the gospel narrative, John called these people 'antichrist,' which is the Greek word *antichristos,* which means 'an opponent of the Messiah.' Also, when we read John's first letter, I believe he is intentionally emphasizing the physical attributes of Jesus to show the fallacy of Gnostic ideology."

> That which was from the beginning, which we have *heard,* which we have *seen with our eyes,* which we have *looked at* and *our hands have touched*—this we proclaim concerning the Word of life. (1John 1:1; emphasis added)

"This is so different. So you're telling me there won't be a future antichrist that will set himself up in a rebuilt temple? I heard they have plans to rebuild the temple though."

The Missing Rebuilt Temple

"The problem with the idea of the temple being rebuilt is the New Testament only speaks of the temple's destruction, never it's reconstruction." Jesus said the temple of stone would be left desolate [Matt. 23:38], and the temple would be taken down one stone upon another [Matt. 24:2]. Also, it doesn't make sense to me that the temple of stone would ever be reconstructed because the Bible teaches in the New

Covenant the temple is not made of stone, it's made of believers in Jesus Christ like you and me [1 Cor. 6:19; 2 Cor. 6:16; Eph. 2:19–22; 1 Pet. 2:5].

Gary Demar writes, "Jesus's completed redemptive work makes the need for a rebuilt temple unnecessary. His ministry begins with the declaration that He is our tabernacle [John 1:14], 'the lamb of God who takes away the sin of the world' [1:29], 'the temple' [John 2:19–21], and the 'chief cornerstone' [Matt. 21:42; Acts 4:11; Eph. 2:20]."[5]

"That makes sense. You know I believe what your saying, I just have never thought about it this in-depth before. Now, can we finally get to the passages about the rapture I have been asking about? I've been dying to know," shes said.

"Yes, it's time we find out what these passages mean once and for all."

[5.] Gary DeMar, What Does the Bible Say About Rebuilding the Temple, Accessed November 15, 2017, http://audio.elparazim.com/BasicsOfBibleProphecy/materials/Lesson_03/What%20Does%20the%20Bible%20Say%20About%20a%20Rebuilt%20Temple.pdf

CHAPTER 7

The Rapture Passages

"First off, let's just read the most popular passage used to defend the pre-tribulation rapture of the church so we can hear what it says and what it doesn't say."

> Brothers and sisters, we do not want you to be uninformed about those who sleep in death, so that you do not grieve like the rest of mankind, who have no hope. For we believe that Jesus died and rose again, and so we believe that God will bring with Jesus those who have fallen asleep in him. According to the Lord's word, we tell you that we who are still alive, who are left until the coming of the Lord, will certainly not precede those who have fallen asleep. For the Lord himself will come down from heaven, with a loud command, with the voice of the archangel and

with the trumpet call of God, and the dead in Christ will rise first. After that, we who are still alive and are left will be caught up together with them in the clouds to meet the Lord in the air. And so we will be with the Lord forever. Therefore encourage one another with these words. (1 Thess. 4:13–18)

"Mom, did you see anything about the church being removed from the earth prior to a seven-year tribulation period?"

"Well, not exactly, but I do know Paul uses the Greek word *harpazo* for the statement 'caught up.' It means 'to take suddenly'. That must be talking about the rapture, right?"

"I don't question that Paul is referencing people being 'caught up' here. That much is clear. What I do question is the idea that this passage is also referring to the *church* being raptured, prior to a seven-year tribulation period. I think sometimes we forget that the pre-tribulation rapture view includes a very large sequence of events and people. If a secret rapture were the only tenet of this belief system, I would agree this passage undeniably could be referring to such an event. The problem comes when we start to pull in the other events and people involved in this belief system. Where does Paul specifically say that it is 'the church' that is caught up? Where is 'the antichrist'? Where is the 'seven-year tribulation period'? Where does Paul say that the antichrist will make a three-and-a-half-year covenant with Israel? Where does Paul say that 'the antichrist' will break that covenant with Israel after the three and a half years? Where does it say the temple will be rebuilt? The truth is Paul doesn't mention any of these key events or people in this passage. If the pre-tribulation rapture is taught in the New Testament, I don't see it taught here or anywhere in the New Testament. Did you know that even Tim Lahaye, co-creator of the Left Behind series even stated in one of his books that there are no Bible verses that teach the the pre, mid, or post-tribulation rapture?"

"You have to be kidding me, are you serious?"

"I am not making it up. Let me read the quote:

'One objection to the pre-tribulation rapture is that not one passage of Scripture teaches the two aspects of His Second Coming separated by the tribulation. This is true. But then, no one passage teaches a post-trib or mid-trib rapture, either.'"[1]

"So why did he teach this belief is true if the Bible doesn't clearly teach it?"

"Your guess is as good as mine, Mom. I know Tim Lahaye was a very kind Christian man and did many good things for the faith, and I honor his heart to help others. Where we must part ways is in believing the pre-tribulation rapture, or any rapture view for that matter since they all are centered around removing the church somewhere around the great tribulation period. We already showed that the great tribulation was a localized tribulation in first century Jerusalem, so thus any belief system that places the great tribulation in the future doesn't seem to fit with the context. I need more biblical evidence before I can believe it."

"If First Thessalonians 4:13–18 is not referring to a pre-tribulation rapture, what is it referring to? How do you explain the being caught up?"

"Well, prior to the 1800s, this passage was understood by biblical scholars to be referencing the general resurrection and the final coming of the Lord

> Prior to the 1800s, this passage was understood by biblical scholars to be referencing the general resurrection and the final coming of the Lord at the end of time. Nobody believed this was referring to some sort of removal of the church from the earth, just prior to a seven-year tribulation period.

---

[1]. LaHaye, Tim F. No Fear of the Storm: Why Christians Will Escape All the Tribulation. Sisters, Oregon: Multnomah Books, 1994.

at the end of time.[2] Nobody believed this was referring to some sort of removal of the church from the earth, just prior to a seven-year tribulation period."

"Do you think it's the same for First Corinthians 15:51–52?"

"Yes, I believe that passage is also talking about the final return of Christ and resurrection at the end of time, the language is practically identical in both passages. That's been the historical belief since the early church."

"You're right, none of those key things are in this passage. I don't get it, though. How could the church be so wrong on such an important subject for so many years? I just don't see how millions of people could believe something the Bible never teaches."

"I've got two words for you, Mom."

"Which words?"

"Protestant Reformation."

"I've heard of that. But what does that mean?"

"In the Protestant Reformation, the issue was over salvation by faith versus works. The church had gotten salvation, the most important part of Christianity, backwards. If we can miss it on salvation, we certainly can miss it on something like prophecy. In 1517, Luther wrote a document called *The Ninety-Five Theses* that challenged the Catholic Church on their view of salvation and the Scriptures. He wrote that the Bible is the central religious authority, and that humans can reach salvation only by faith, and not by works. This started a reformation. I believe there is another reformation happening with the church that includes believers studying the Bible for themselves to see what they believe about the end-times and other subjects."[3]

[2.] See Matthew Henry Commentary on the Whole Bible, John Gill's Exposition of the Bible, Joseph Benson's Commentary of the Old and New Testaments, Albert Barnes' Notes on the Whole Bible, Matthew Pool's Commentary on the Holy Bible, Jamieson-Fausset-Brown Commentary Critical and Explanatory on the Whole Bible, Wesley's Explanatory Notes, and The Geneva Study Bible.

[3.] Martin Luther and the 95 Theses, Accessed November 15, 2017, http://www.history.com/topics/martin-luther-and-the-95-theses.

"Well, I am considering what you're saying, but I still have one huge question. If the end-times are not full of tribulation, what are we waiting on before Jesus comes back?"

"I can tell you my view of the end-times in one word: Kingdom"

"What exactly does that mean?"

"Let's look at what the Bible says about the Kingdom, and then it will all make sense."

> I can tell you my view of the end-times in one word: Kingdom

CHAPTER 8

The Kingdom

THE KINGDOM TIMELINE

3 BC — Birth of Jesus Messiah.

AD 27 — Baptism. Jesus' ministry begins.

AD 30 — Crucified. Resurrected. New Covenant begins.

+7 WEEKS — Pentecost. Holy Spirit arrives.

AD 67 — Jewish-Roman War begins.

AD 70 — Romans annihilate Jerusalem and Temple. Old Covenant ends.

© 2017 J.A. Hardgrave Graphic by Saint Logo

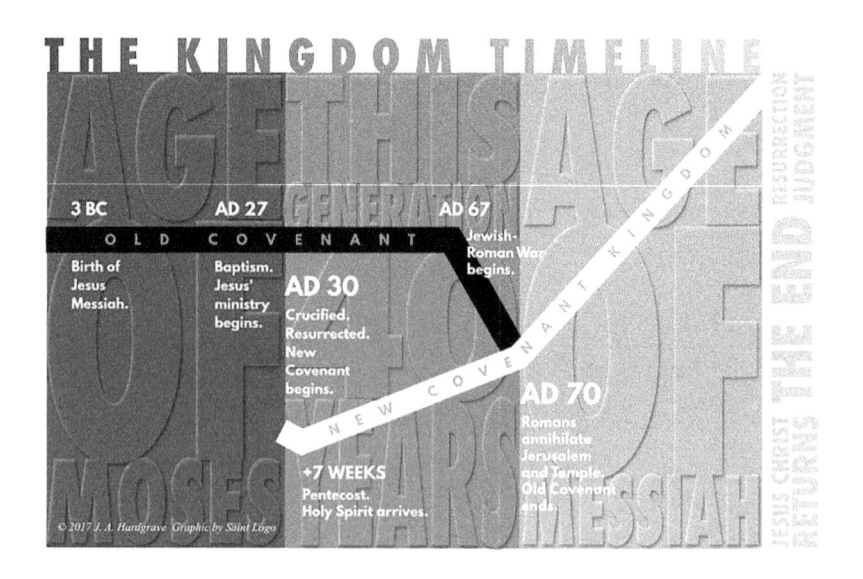

"Mom, let's look at a few events that have happened and a few events that have not happened. Jesus was born in about 3 BC. In AD 27, He was baptized and went around preaching and demonstrating the gospel of the Kingdom. During His ministry, the Old Covenant age was in full force with animal sacrifices still being offered. In AD 30, Jesus was crucified, and His blood made a new and better covenant. Three days later, He resurrected and appeared to many for fifty days and spoke about the Kingdom of God [Acts 1:3]. Then Jesus poured out the Holy Spirit in the upper room, and the Kingdom (which is the empowerment to rule and reign with Christ) came upon the church. Although the New Covenant had arrived through Christ's perfect sacrifice, animal sacrifices would continue for forty more years until the temple was destroyed in AD 70. As the writer of Hebrews put it, God was removing the shakable kingdom since an unshakable kingdom had arrived through His Spirit [Heb. 12:18–29]."

"Now we are in the age of the Messiah and Jesus is ruling and reigning until all His enemies have been put under His feet [1 Cor. 15:25]. His Kingdom is spiritual since it comes through the Holy Spirit ([Rom. 14:17; Acts 1:6;—8)], and don't forget Jesus said the Kingdom is within us (Luke 17:21) which means the Kingdom can't be literal since a literal Kingdom that includes a temple of stone and a literal throne can't fit inside us. However, God's Spirit can fit inside us and is producing the fruit of righteousness, joy, and peace that I believe will continue to spread through all the nations until Jesus returns. Jesus said the Kingdom is like a mustard seed. It starts small, but it grows into the largest tree in the field [Matt. 13:31].

Because of the expanding reality of the Kingdom, we should be believing for the Kingdom to come on earth as it is in heaven [Matt. 6:10]. We should expect more and more people to enter a relationship with King Jesus. We should expect the church to rise in victory and power as we unite in our common pursuit of Jesus. We should expect our relationships to flourish as we bear the fruit of the Spirit by loving God and loving people in community. My friend Jamie Englehart puts our Kingdom mission this way: 'The first Adam turned a garden into a graveyard but the last Adam (Jesus) came to turn a graveyard back into a garden. Mary thought Jesus was the gardener. Well, He was. The gardener had returned'" [John 20:13–16].

"Jesus said as believers, we have received the keys to the Kingdom of heaven which means we already have heaven's backing and empowerment to bring heaven to earth. The first Adam forfeited the keys, the last Adam (Jesus) won the keys of the Kingdom back and then handed them to the church, which is God's representative in the earth [2 Cor. 5:20; Matt. 16:19]. What if Jesus came to communicate that it's time for us as the church to pick up where He left off and for us to

> What if the goal of Jesus was not just to get us from earth to heaven after we die, but to empower us to bring heaven to earth before we die?

restore the planet back into a paradise as the new gardeners of the earth? What if the goal of Jesus was not just to get us from earth to heaven after we die, but to empower us to bring heaven to earth before we die? I believe Jesus wants to partner with us and use us to transform the earth with the reality of heaven. We now have the empowerment to live like Jesus did, and I believe God is calling us back to a Christian life that looks more like the book of Acts than a religious institution. As my friend, Pastor Josh Adkins from The Loft Church[1] says, "Christ unveiled a different possibility, a kingdom of heaven on earth reality that is not only possible to engage but should become the new operating system by which every born-again person functions." The Loft Church is one of many churches that are rising up with this Kingdom commission to bring revival and restoration to all the nations of the world. Once the Kingdom has fully been advanced in the earth, I believe at that point, time and eternity will merge, and then three things will happen."

1) The final bodily return of Jesus Christ (Acts 1:9–11; 1 Thess. 4:13–18)
2) The Final Resurrection (1 Thess. 4:13–18; 1 Cor. 15:51–52)
3) The Final Judgment (John 5:29)

"Wow, that is certainly what I believe. I am so excited about the future now! It finally clicked for me after you laid that out. Now I have something to really believe for. I have to tell you, after all our talks, I now have more understanding about the end-times than ever before. I even have a new joy when I think about the future. I feel like I've got so much time left, whereas before I felt as though at any moment, the world was going to end. I have had people talk about the end-times around me, and now I finally have something to say. I've already seen many people really be impacted. I go into the Scriptures, and many of them make sense now that I see what they meant to the original audience. I'm sorry I was so harsh. I just had no idea or understanding the end-times could be so simple. It's just

---

[1] http://www.loft.church/

tough admitting I had believed something that wasn't biblical. I do have to tell you though—I do find it hard to believe things will get better and better when the world is worse than ever."

"Are you sure about that, Mom?"

"I am pretty sure. Look at the news."

"What if I told you that in many ways the world is the best it has ever been in human history?"

"I would say I don't believe you."

"Let me read you some statistics I found. Prepare to be surprised. Sadly, you don't hear about these things in the news."

World Christianity

A comprehensive demographic study of more than 200 countries finds that there are 2.18 billion Christians of all ages around the world, representing nearly a third of the estimated 2010 global population of 6.9 billion.[2]

The number of Christians around the world has nearly quadrupled in the last 100 years, from about 600 million in 1910 to more than 2 billion in 2010.[3]

Christianity has grown enormously in sub-Saharan Africa and the Asia-Pacific region, where there were relatively few Christians at the beginning of the 20th century. The share of the population that is Christian in sub-Saharan Africa climbed from 9% in 1910 to 63% in 2010, while in the Asia-Pacific region it rose from 3% to 7%.

---

[2] Global Christianity – A Report on the Size and Distribution of the World's Christian Population, Pew Forum on Religion and Public Life, Pew Research Center, Dec. 2011.

[3] Ibid.

Christianity today – unlike a century ago – is truly a global faith. [4]

Although Christians comprise just under a third of the world's people, they form a majority of the population in 158 countries and territories, about two-thirds of all the countries and territories in the world. [5]

About 90% of Christians live in countries where Christians are in the majority; only about 10% of Christians worldwide live as minorities.[6]

In 1910 the number of Christians in the Americas was 165.9 million. In 2010, the number had climbed to 804.1 million. This is a 385% increase.[7]

Mom, we are also seeing a significant rise in the number of those who believe in the gifts of the Spirit being for today which I think you would agree is part of the Kingdom growing since the Kingdom comes through the Spirit moving through the church.

Based on survey results, Pentecostals and Charismatics together make up 23% of the population in the USA. In Brazil the percentage is 49%; 44% in the Philippines; and 56% of the population in Kenya.[8]

As a percent of all Protestants, Pentecostals and Charismatics make up 28% in the USA; 78% of Protestants in Brazil; 73% in Brazil; and 67% in the Philippines.[9]

[4.] Ibid.
[5.] Ibid.
[6.] Ibid.
[7.] Ibid.
[8.] Spirit and Power, A 10-Country Survey of Pentecostals, Pew Forum on Religion and Public Life, Pew Research Center, Oct, 2006.
[9.] Ibid.

World Evangelism

Every day another 74,000 people across the globe come to faith in Christ. That's 3,083 new fellow believers every hour of every day.[10]

More than three billion people have viewed Christian films such as the Jesus film—which has been shown in 228 countries, with 197,298,327 viewers indicating a commitment to Christ.[11]

In 1950, when China was closed to foreign missionaries, there were one million believers in the country. Today conservative estimates say there are well over 80 million. An average of 28,000 people become believers every day in the People's Republic of China.[12]

In AD 100 there were 360 non-Christians per true believer. Today the ratio is less than seven to every believer as the initiative of the Holy Spirit continues to outstrip our most optimistic plans! Throughout history the growth of the body of Christ has outdistanced the increase of world population.[13]

---

[10] Bill and Amy Stearns, Vision 2020, Amazing Stories of What God is Doing Around the World, Bethany House Publishers, Jan. 2005, from World Evangelism Statistics, and Missions Giving, Randy Alcorn, July 17, 2008, Accessed November 14, 2017, http://www.epm.org/blog/2008/Jul/17/world-evangelism-statistics-and-missions-giving.
[11] Ibid.
[12] Ibid.
[13] Ibid.

Life Expectancy

Average life expectancy at birth in 1955 was just 48 years; in 1995 it was 65 years; in 2025 it will reach 73 years. By the year 2025, it is expected that no country will have a life expectancy of less than 50 years. Over 5 billion people in 120 countries today have life expectancy of more than 60 years.[14]

Reducing Child Mortality

Overall, substantial progress has been made towards reducing child mortality. The number of under-five deaths worldwide has declined from 12.7 (12.6, 13.0) million in 1990 to 5.9 (5.7, 6.4) million in 2015. This translates into 19,000 fewer children dying every day in 2015 than in 1990. The remarkable decline in under-five mortality since 2000 has saved the lives of 48 million children under age five—children who would not have survived to see their fifth birthday if the under-five mortality rate from 2000 onward remained at the same level as in 2000.[15]

Between 2000 and 2016, the number of children involved in hazardous work conditions and performing child labor has been reduced by more than 50%. As we head to a world of low-cost robotics, where such machines can operate far faster, far cheaper and around the clock, the basic rationale for child labor will completely

---

[14.] World Health Report 1998, World Health Organization.
[15.] Global Health Observatory, World Health Organization.

disappear, and projections anticipate that it will drop to zero.[16]

Economic Prosperity

Absolute poverty is defined as living on less than $1.25/day. Over the last 30 years, the share of the global population living in absolute poverty has declined from 53% to under 17%.[17]

Over the last 50 years, the percent of our disposable income spent on food has dropped by more than 50 percent, from 14% to less than 6%. This is largely a function of better food production technology, distribution processes and policies that have reduced the cost of food.[18]

Literacy Rates

World literacy rates from 1820 to 2010 grew from 12% of the population to 83%. In the developed world the literacy rate approaches 100%. In the US, 99% of the population is considered literate. In countries with lower rates of literacy, the

---

[16.] International Labor Organization, from "Why the World Is Better Than You Think in 10 Powerful Charts," Peter Diamandis, June 27, 2016. Accessed November 13, 2017, https://singularityhub.com/2016/06/27/why-the-world-is-better-than-you-think-in-10-powerful-charts.

[17.] Our World in Data, Max Roser, from Why the World Is Better Than You Think in 10 Powerful Charts, Peter Diamandis, June 27, 2016, Accessed November 13, 2017, https://singularityhub.com/2016/06/27/why-the-world-is-better-than-you-think-in-10-powerful-charts.

[18.] USDA, Economic Research Service, Food Expenditure Series, from Why the World Is Better Than You Think in 10 Powerful Charts, Peter Diamandis, June 27, 2016, Accessed November 13, 2017, https://singularityhub.com/2016/06/27/why-the-world-is-better-than-you-think-in-10-powerful-charts.

most dramatic growth is in younger age groups, which is a direct benefit of improved educational programs.[19]

War

The number of war deaths has plummeted. In the 1950s, there were almost 250 deaths caused by war per million people. Now, there are less than 10 per million.[20]

During 2012—the most recent year for which there are data—the number of conflicts being waged around the world dropped sharply, from 37 to 32. High–intensity conflicts have declined by more than half since the end of the Cold War, while terrorism, genocide and homicide numbers are also down. The number of international wars has fallen hard since the 1950s (from more than six a year, to less than one a year now).[21]

The number of people per million (total global population) who have died in armed conflict dropped from 235 in 1950 to 2.5 in 2007, despite an increase in the number of smaller conflicts.[22]

---

[19]. Max Roser and Esteban Ortiz-Ospina, 'Literacy', Published online at OurWorldInData.org, 2017. Accessed November 15, 2017, https://ourworldindata.org/literacy/).

[20]. Colin Schultz, Globally, Deaths from War and Murder Are in Decline, The world is getting safer, even if it doesn't necessarily feel like it, March 21, 2014, Accessed November 15, 2017, https://www.smithsonianmag.com/smart-news/globally-deaths-war-and-murder-are-decline-180950237.

[21]. Ibid.

[22]. Andrew Cohen, The World is Getting Worse (and Other Lies), Accessed November 14, 2017, http://bigthink.com/the-evolution-of-enlightenment/the-world-is-getting-worse-and-other-lies.

Crime

As recent as the early 80s and mid-90s, there were over 50 violent crime victims per 1,000 individuals. Recently, this number has dropped threefold to 15 victims per 1,000 people. We continue to make our country (and the world) a safer place to live.[23]

The number of burglaries per 1000 population in the USA has dropped from 110 in 1973 to 26 in 2008. This is a 76% decrease.[24]

From 1991 to 2014, the rate of violent crime in the USA dropped from 758 per 100,000 to 375/100,000 population. This is a 50% decrease.[25]

Health and Disease

Between 2010 and 2015, malaria incidence among populations at risk (the rate of new cases) fell by 21% globally. In that same period, malaria mortality rates among populations at risk fell by 29% globally among all age groups, and by 35% among children under 5.[26]

Many infectious diseases have been virtually eradicated in the USA. The following percentages

---

[23] Gallup, Bureau of Justice Statistics, from Why the World Is Better Than You Think in 10 Powerful Charts, Peter Diamandis, June 27, 2016, Accessed November 13, 2017, https://singularityhub.com/2016/06/27/why-the-world-is-better-than-you-think-in-10-powerful-charts.

[24] Bureau of Justice Statistics, Office of Justice Programs, www.ojp.usdoj.gov.

[25] Uniform Crime Reporting Statistics, FBI, US Dept. of Justice, https://www.ucrdatatool.gov.

[26] Malaria Fact Sheet, Media Center, World Health Organization, April 2017 Accessed November 16, 2017, http://www.who.int/mediacentre/factsheets/fs094/en/.

represent the reductions in these diseases: Polio 100%, Rubella 99%, Measles 99%, Mumps 99%, Pertussis 93%, H Influenza 99%, Hepatitis A 91%, Hepatitis B 83%, Pneumococcal Disease 74%.[27]

Thanks to immunization and advances in public sanitation, the incidence of typhoid fever in developed countries has been reduced to about five cases per one million people per year.[28]

India hails polio-free 'milestone'. India has eliminated polio.[29]

In the 18th and 19th centuries, smallpox was a worldwide endemic disease that was a leading cause of death. Following a concerted worldwide effort at immunization, the deadly disease was completely eradicated in 1979.[30]

America's teen birth rate has plummeted at an unprecedented rate, falling faster and faster. Between 2007 and 2013, the number of babies born to teens annually fell by 38.4 percent, according to research firm Demographic Intelligence. This drop occurred in tandem with steep declines in the abortion rate. That suggests that the drop isn't the product of more teenag-

---

[27]. Tara Culp-Ressler, Center for Disease Control from Vaccines Have Almost Totally Eliminated These 13 Infectious Diseases in the U.S., Feb. 22, 2013, Thinkprogress.org.

[28]. Brian Childs, "10 Deadly Diseases that Have Been Eliminated in the U.S.," Brian Childs, December 11, 2013, Accessed November 13, 2017, https://masterpublichealth.com/10-deadly-diseases-that-have-been-eliminated-in-the-u-s.

[29]. India hails polio-free milestone, BBC.com, Jan. 13, 2014. http://www.bbc.com/news/world-asia-india-25708715.

[30]. Brian Childs, "10 Deadly Diseases that Have Been Eliminated in the U.S.," Brian Childs, December 11, 2013, Accessed November 13, 2017, https://masterpublichealth.com/10-deadly-diseases-that-have-been-eliminated-in-the-u-s.

ers terminating pregnancies. More simply, fewer girls are getting pregnant.[31]

Percent of persons who failed to obtain needed medical care due to cost: 4.4%

Percent with a usual place to go for medical care: 88.1%[32]

Internet Access and Cell Phones

We can now access any information on the planet in an instant as well as communicate with people from around the world instantly. This is a reality that was foreign and impossible to previous generations.

The number of internet users has increased tenfold from 1999 to 2013. The first billion was reached in 2005; the second billion in 2010; the third billion in 2014.[33]

Rates of penetration vary across the world from a high of 88% having access to the internet in North America to a low of 31% in Africa. In 2017 approximately 3.8 billion people had internet access, which is 51% of the world population.[34]

In the late 1990's, countries in North America and Western Europe were the first areas to begin rapid adoption of mobile phones, with

---

[31] Sarah Kliff, 'The Mystery of the Falling Teen Birth Rate,' Vox.com Jan. 21, 2015. Accessed November 15, 2017, https://www.vox.com/2014/8/20/5987845/the-mystery-of-the-falling-teen-birth-rate.

[32] Access to Health Care, Fast Stats, National Center for Health Statistics, Center for Disease Control, Accessed November 16, 2017, https://www.cdc.gov/nchs/fastats/access-to-health-care.htm.

[33] Internet Users, http://www.internetlivestats.com/internet-users.

[34] Usage and Population Statistics, http://www.internetworldstats.com/stats.htm.

many countries in Western Europe reaching almost 100% penetration by 2003. More recently over the last 10 years, mobile phone adoption in countries in South America, North Africa, and the Middle East grew as the technology became available in these more developing markets. By 2013, many countries across the world surpassed 100% market penetration, with many individuals now owning more than one mobile phone. Notable countries that are still lagging include North Korea, Myanmar, and several countries in central Africa. The International Telecommunications Union (ITU) estimated global mobile phone subscriptions reached almost 7 billion in 2014, and the growth in penetration over the past two decades reflects how integrated these devices have become in our lives.[35]

New Technology

A bodybuilder who was born color-blind was able to see color for the first time when his family surprised him on his 66th birthday. The glasses enabled the man to see color via corrective lenses. When he put on the corrective lenses, he began to cry with amazement of the colors surrounding him.[36]

---

[35] Samuel Kornstein, 'The Rise of Mobile Phones: 20 Years of Global Adoption', June 29, 2015. Accessed November 16, 2017, https://blog.cartesian.com/the-rise-of-mobile-phones-20-years-of-global-adoption.

[36] Amanda Prestigiacomo, www.dailywire.com, Sept 17, 2017. http://www.dailywire.com/news/21180/video-66-year-old-bodybuilder-seeing-color-first-amanda-prestigiacomo.

A new technology that translates language in real-time, is now available. The ear pieces and software app, translate in 40 languages.[37]

Brackish wells (wells that have salty and unclean water) are everywhere around the world. And while brackish water isn't as salty as ocean water, it's still too salty to drink or to use for irrigation. The RainMaker for Brackish Water is a filtration unit that removes the salts and other minerals from brackish water and makes it suitable for both human consumption and agriculture. The device is intended for use at the village level. It simply attaches to the well and starts working immediately, cleaning water at a rate of 5–10 gallons per minute. And unlike other water filtration devices, this one uses very little energy. It takes just 1.5 kilowatts, which is about as much as a hair dryer, so a small generator can power it. If enough brackish water can be turned into fresh water, the water crisis in some regions can be delayed for several years, if not decades.[38]

In 1960, Americans owned 61,671,390 passenger cars, or about one car for every three people.

In 2008, Americans owned 137,079,843 passenger cars, or a little less than one car for every two people.

Worldwide, car ownership has been increasing. As developing countries attain greater economic stability, their residents are more likely to purchase vehicles. Today, consumers in China,

---

[37] www.itranslate.com/ear-translator.
[38] https://billionsinchange.com/solutions/water/.

India, and other Asian markets play a significant role in worldwide automotive consumption.[39]

"Jordan, this is life-changing! You never hear about these amazing things on the news, they make it seem like nothing is going right in the world. Maybe the world isn't so bad after all. My eyes are truly being opened. So, Jesus must be coming soon since so many things are going well, right?"

"Well, here's the truth. The world is much better than most people realize. This may be the safest time to be alive in human history. However, there is still much work to be done. There are many ways to advance the Kingdom, but here are just a few Kingdom opportunities for us to consider."

Kingdom Opportunities in Christianity

Pastor James McDonald from Walking in the Word Ministries revealed these shocking numbers about Christianity in America. Of the 250,000 Protestant churches in America, 200,000 are either stagnant (with no growth) or declining. That is 80% of the churches in America and maybe the one you attend, if you attend at all. 4,000 churches close their doors every single year. There is less than half of the number of churches today than there were only 100 years ago. 3,500 people leave the church every single day. Since 1950, there are 1/3rd fewer churches in the U.S.[40]

[39.] Car Ownership Statistics, Accessed November 16, 2017, http://cars.lovetoknow.com/Car_Ownership_Statistics.

[40.] Jack Wellman, "Why We Are Losing So Many Churches in the United States," Christian Crier, Oct. 23, 2013. Accessed November 15, 2017, http://www.patheos.com/blogs/christiancrier/2013/10/26/why-we-are-losing-so-many-churches-in-the-united-states/

55,000 people die daily in India and around the world without ever hearing the True Name.[41]

86% of Buddhists, Hindus, and Muslims do not know a Christian personally and only 25% of all African non-Christians, know a Christian.[42]

There are more than 45,000 different Christian denominations in the world today. In 1900 there were 1600 denominations. This is a 2,712 percent increase in the division of the Church in just over a century. Most of the denominations that exist are due to disputes, usually over doctrine but frequently over personal conflict.[43]

As the Millennial generation enters adulthood, its members display much lower levels of religious affiliation, including less connection with Christian churches, than older generations. Fully 36% of young Millennials (those between the ages of 18 and 24) are religiously unaffiliated, as are 34% of older Millennials (ages 25-33). And fewer than six-in-ten Millennials identify with any branch of Christianity, compared with seven-in-ten or more among older generations, including Baby Boomers and Gen-Xers. Just 16% of Millennials are Catholic, and only 11%

---

[41] Bill and Amy Stearns, Vision 2020, Amazing Stories of What God is Doing Around the World, Bethany House Publishers, Jan. 2005, from World Evangelism Statistics, and Missions Giving, Randy Alcorn, July 17, 2008, Accessed November 14, 2017, http://www.epm.org/blog/2008/Jul/17/world-evangelism-statistics-and-missions-giving

[42] Christianity in its Global Context, 1970–2020 Society, Religion, and Mission, Center for the Study of Global Christianity June 2013, http://www.gordonconwell.edu/ockenga/research/documents/christianityinitsglobalcontext.pdf

[43] Krish Kandiah, 'The Church is Growing, and Here Are the Figures That Prove It', Christian Today, March 5, 2015. Accessed November 17, 2017, https://www.christiantoday.com/article/a-growing-church-why-we-should-focus-on-the-bigger-picture/49362.htm.

identify with mainline Protestantism. Roughly one-in-five are evangelical Protestants.[44]

Whereas 85% of the silent generation (born 1928-1945) call themselves Christians, just 56% of today's younger millennials (born 1990-1996) do the same, even though the vast majority—about eight in 10—were raised in religious homes. Each successive generation of Americans includes fewer Christians, Pew has found.

To put it simply: Older generations of Americans are not passing along the Christian faith as effectively as their forebears.[45]

Data from the Southern Baptist Convention indicates that they are currently losing 70–88% of their youth after their freshman year in college. 70% of teenagers involved in church youth groups stop attending church within two years of their high school graduation.[46]

As of 2010, Christianity was by far the world's largest religion, with an estimated 2.2 billion adherents, nearly a third (31%) of all 6.9 billion people on Earth. Islam was second, with 1.6 billion adherents, or 23% of the global population.[47]

If current demographic trends continue, however, Islam will nearly catch up by the middle of the 21st century. Between 2010 and 2050, Muslims—a comparatively youthful population

---

[44] Pew Research Center, "America's Changing Religious Landscape, Religion and Public Life," Pew Research Center, May 2015.

[45] Ibid., from: Millennials Leaving Church in Droves, Study Finds, Daniel Burke, cnn.com, May 14, 2015. Accessed November 17, 2017, http://www.cnn.com/2015/05/12/living/pew-religion-study/index.html.

[46] Southern Baptist Convention Data, from: Remarks to the Southern Baptist Convention Executive Committee, T. C. Pinkney, Nashville, Tennessee, 2001.

[47] Pew Research Center, "The Future of World Religions: Population Growth Projections, 2010--2050, Religion and Public Life," April. 2015.

with high fertility rates—are projected to increase by 73%. The number of Christians also is projected to rise, but more slowly, at about the same rate (35%) as the global population overall. As a result, by 2050 there will be near parity between Muslims (2.8 billion, or 30% of the population) and Christians (2.9 billion, or 31%), possibly for the first time in history.[48]

Kingdom Opportunities in Food Access

The 2016 estimates found that one in nine people suffers from chronic hunger and in 2014, 12.9 percent of the population in developing countries was undernourished.[49]

Every day too many men and women across the globe struggle to feed their children a nutritious meal. In a world where we produce enough food to feed everyone, 815 million people – one in nine – still go to bed on an empty stomach each night. Even more, one in three, suffer from some form of malnutrition.[50]

There is some good news about food access though.

By 2030, only 1 in 7 people are expected to be consuming less than 2,500 calories per day.

---

[48]. Ibid.
[49]. Food Security, Understanding Poverty, World Bank. Accessed November 17, 2017, http://www.worldbank.org/en/topic/food-security.
[50]. Zero Hunger, World Food Program. Accessed November 17, 2017, http://www1.wfp.org/zero-hunger.

This is great news— it means more people in developing countries are eating more![51]

Kingdom Opportunities in Human Trafficking

There are more human slaves in the world today than ever before in history.[52]

There are an estimated 27 million adults and 13 million children around the world who are victims of human trafficking.[53]

There are more than three million prostitutes in India. 40% are children under 18.[54]

The FBI estimates that over 100,000 children and young women are trafficked in America today. They range in age from nine to 19, with the average being age 11. Many victims are not just runaways or abandoned, but are from "good" families who are coerced by clever traffickers.[55]

Belgium, Germany, Greece, Israel, Italy, Japan, the Netherlands, Thailand, Turkey, and the U.S. are ranked very high as destination countries of trafficked victims. Women are trafficked to the U.S. largely to work in the sex industry (including strip clubs, peep and touch shows, massage parlors that offer sexual services, and prostitution).

[51.] Jordan Elton, "14 Surprising Stats about Global Food Consumption", November 12, 2014, Accessed November 17, 2017, https://www.one.org/us/2014/11/12/14-surprising-stats-about-global-food-consumption.

[52.] E. Benjamin. Skinner, E. Benjamin. *A Crime So Monstrous: Face-to-Face with Modern-Day Slavery*, New York, NY: Free Press, 2008.).

[53.] Ibid.

[54.] http://www.mattsorger.com/missions/india-missions/rescue1-sponsorship-program.

[55.] "Teen Girls Stories of Sex Trafficking in the U.S.," ABC News/Primetime. February 9, 2006. Accessed November 17, 2017, http://abcnews.go.com/Primetime/story?id=1596778&page=1.

They are also trafficked to work in sweatshops, domestic servitude, and agricultural work.[56]

(If you want to get involved with a trusted Kingdom ministry that is actively trying to end sex trafficking, I highly recommend connecting with Matt Sorger Ministries. You can see their mission and become a part of it by visiting Rescue1now.com)

"I had no idea all that stuff was going on. We have so much to do. I almost pray Jesus will hold off on coming so we can bring change in the world!"

"I agree, Mom. Once we see that the Kingdom of God is here but has not advanced throughout the whole earth, we see our responsibility to get busy.

Notice that even though the Kingdom of God was present when Jesus was in ministry, the whole earth did not immediately become influenced by it.

Jesus had to go around and release the Kingdom into people's lives through the power of the Holy Spirit. Don't forget, we have an entire book of the Bible called "Acts". The early followers of Jesus did something with what they received and with only a limited number of them they still managed to, "Turn the world upside down" (Acts 17:6).

The truth is Jesus did not come to earth to set up a religion where we sit down and go through all the formalities. Jesus came to set up a spiritual kingdom where His followers would rule and reign and make earth like heaven.

[56.] Skinner, *A Crime So Monstrous*.

However, this kingdom advancement doesn't happen automatically. That's why I believe the Kingdom is likened by Jesus to a small mustard seed that grows. The Kingdom within us usually flows out onto people one or two at a time, and slowly but surely people experience a breakthrough and turn to King Jesus.

Many people hear that the Kingdom is present and think, "That's impossible, look how bad the world is!". That's because we haven't recognized the Kingdom is ever expanding and doesn't come all at once. If that were the case, as soon as Jesus received the Holy Spirit, the entire world would have been saved, healed, delivered, and in right relationship with God.

Jesus knew He couldn't advance the Kingdom alone in His lifetime. That's why He said, "But in fact, it is best for you that I go away, because if I don't, the Advocate won't come. If I do go away, then I will send him to you (John 16:7).

Jesus knew that one Man full of the Spirit of God could bring some transformation, but He knew that millions and billions of believers full of His Spirit could bring global transformation —that's why He wanted to leave and send His Spirit.

I don't believe Jesus is coming soon, because His bodily return is determined by how much the Kingdom has advanced in the earth, and there's still way too much advancement to be done. The question is, what are we going to do with what we now know? The world is waiting for the sons and daughters of God to rise and bring transformation in whatever area God has given us influence. It's not time to wait, —it's time to reign."

7 KEYS TO A HEALTHY DISCUSSION OF SCRIPTURE

Here are seven keys to a healthy discussion of Scripture that will serve as a guide during your conversations. I made many mistakes when I first began discussing prophecy and the Kingdom with people. I was very excited and passionate but realized how we say things is just as important as what we say. You may be wondering if we are even called to have such discussions of Scripture.

Peter told us to "always be ready to give an answer to everyone who asks you to give the reason for the hope that you have" (1 Pet. 3:15). Paul said we should "demolish arguments and every pretension that sets itself up against the knowledge of God" (2 Cor. 10:5). Titus said that to be part of his church leadership, someone "must hold firmly to the trustworthy message as it has been taught, so that he can encourage others by sound doctrine and refute those who oppose it" (Titus 1:9). Jude urged believers to "contend for the faith that was once for all entrusted to God's holy people" (Jude 1:3). After reading this book, I believe you have already been equipped with enough truth to make a convincing case for a present Kingdom and an optimistic future. You don't have to be a prophecy expert to ask convincing questions and share the basics. But remember, the primary reason Jesus died was not to make us scholars and debaters, but to make us sons and daughters. Our primary goal is not to debate the Kingdom, but demonstrate the Kingdom through our lives. If we find ourselves doing more debating than demonstrating, I believe we have gotten off track and should focus more on impacting those around us with the Holy Spirit who lives within us. With that being said, I do believe there is a power in boldly declaring truth to people so here are 7 keys I have found to a healthy discussion of Scripture

1) **Always remain in love.**

Love supersedes doctrine. Our goal should be to win the person, not the argument. We must move from a desire to be a right, to a desire to find the truth and do so in a way that's loving. Paul's method was to be "all things to all men" (1 Cor. 9:19–23). This meant he always kept the other person in mind in his evangelistic efforts. I have learned to make my approach tailor-made to the person I am speaking with based upon what they are comfortable with. Some are going to be just like I was, asking questions and ready for answers. Others are going to be a bit more skeptical, so remaining in love is critical. Prophecy is often a very tense subject as it is, so speaking with a tone of love will help to keep the conversation productive and focused on finding truth.

2) **Stay tethered to the text.**

Charles Spurgeon once said, "Defend the Bible? I would as soon defend a lion! Unchain it and it will defend itself." He's right. Our job is not to defend the Scriptures, our job is to present the Scriptures in context and let them convince the skeptics. The truth speaks for itself and doesn't need too much help if we present it in context. I used to get very uneasy when speaking about my beliefs because I thought it was my job to defend them.

Once I learned to let the Scriptures do all the work, it became quite fun to have discussions. Sometimes the Scriptures confirmed with what I believed, other times the Scriptures showed I had missed it, and I changed my beliefs. During a conversation about Scripture, I will spend a lot of time keeping the focus on the Scriptures by saying "Which verse would you like to discuss?" When the Scriptures stay as the focus, both people will find themselves growing as they both look at the context to discover the meaning.

3) **Always understand what you disagree on before you begin the discussion.**

Many times I have made the mistake of not clarifying what I disagree with someone on before engaging in a biblical discussion. After hours of going in circles, we would end up realizing we never disagreed to begin with. I have found many discussions center around the understanding of Christian terms like *law, grace, obedience, rapture,* etc. We usually believe the same thing but just have a different term for it.

For example, some people accidentally say rapture when they are really referring to the final resurrection and final return of Christ and not a pre-tribulation rapture of Christians. That's why it's important to never assume an understanding based on terminology. If we take the time to confirm what someone believes and doesn't believe before we begin our discussion, it will ensure the conversation is fruitful and progressing toward truth. The best thing to do is ask them the question right up front, "What exactly do we disagree on before we begin our discussion?" It also never hurts to mention something you agree on like you both being brothers or sisters in Christ to create unity.

4) Let the conversations come to you.

"A man convinced against his will is of the same opinion still."

I believe we are called to engage in discussions with people asking questions who are hungry for truth. You usually don't have to go looking for discussions. They will come to you—especially with all the end-of-the-world predictions that are happening more frequently each year. When someone is not ready to discuss something and we try to engage them anyway, we can actually push them away.

Sometimes God will lead you to bring up prophecy or another biblical subject, but I have found it's best to let them come to you. The best way to convince someone who doesn't want to be convinced is to live the values you want to teach them. When it comes to prophecy, show them you are full of hope for the future by making long-term plans. Talk about advancing the Kingdom of God and go out and make a difference. And of course, pray their heart would be softened to hear your view of a present and advancing kingdom.

5) **Expect them to be uncomfortable hearing something they haven't heard before.**

"The truth will make you free, but first it will make you mad." People's end-time view is often sacred, because it's the by-product of years, sometimes decades of teaching, by people they love and trust. When we bring up a different perspective, it becomes personal because of all the elements involved. That's why we must remain in love during our conversations and not be thrown off when people get a little upset.

It's not easy to hear that you have believed something that may not be biblical. It's also not easy to hear that the people you loved and trusted were teaching something that wasn't biblical. As you read in my story, I went through those exact challenges. However, if we can remain in love and plant seeds of truth, I have seen many people come back to me months, or even years, later and tell me they now see what I was saying and have changed their view. I have also spoken with many people who hold the views presented in this book who said that when they first heard it, they were upset, only to study it out and see that it was biblical.

6) **Have a prophecy book, blog, or document pre-prepared.**

One of the first things I did after studying this view of prophecy was to write out a blog that gave an overview of my beliefs. When someone would ask me about prophecy, I found out it was tough to truly capture my beliefs in one sitting. Prophecy involves thousands of verses and hundreds of subjects. Things can get very in-depth quickly. By referring them to a blog, it allowed them to see the bigger picture and a more in-depth presentation without having to remember all the answers during the conversation.

Of course, I would be honored if you give them my book because I have strategically designed it to be a very gentle introduction to this view of prophecy for even the most closed skeptic. The other option is you can write and print out your own overview of prophecy. Just a few pages are fine. Mention the time statements, audience relevance, and just give a basic overview for people to consider. It doesn't take much to get people seeking the truth for themselves if they are hungry enough.

7) **Stay humble.**

I have studied what I presented in this book for several years now, but I still have many subjects related to prophecy that I can't explain. One of the statements I say often when I don't know the answer is "I don't know." We should never feel like we have to have all the answers to have an impact on people. I have only blogged about the subjects I presented in this book and have seen thousands of lives transformed. At this point, I have never once written or talked much about the book of Revelation. Even so, I have learned to focus on what I do know, and not focus on what I don't know. We read in Scripture that knowledge puffs up, but love edifies (1 Cor. 8:1). We can have all the knowledge in the world, but without love, it won't change people's lives. Prophecy is very important and should be studied and talked about, but what's most important is people entering into a relationship with Jesus Christ by hearing the gospel and seeing that love demonstrated through us. No matter what subject we talk about, we should talk about it with love and humility because we are always growing.

RECOMMENDED READING

A Good Overview and Introduction

    Last Days Madness by Gary DeMar
    Surprised by Hope N. T. Wright
    Victorious Eschatology by Harold Eberle and Martin Trench
    The Last Days According to Jesus by R. C. Sproul
    Understanding the Whole Bible by Dr. Jonathan Welton
    Wars and Rumors of Wars by Gary DeMar

Understanding Matthew 24

    Is Jesus Coming Soon? By Gary DeMar
    Victorious Eschatology by Harold Eberle and Martin Trench
    The Great Tribulation by David Chilton
    The Olivet Discourse Made Easy by Kenneth Gentry
    Wars and Rumors of Wars by Gary DeMar
    Understanding the Whole Bible by Dr. Jonathan Welton

The History of the Modern View

    Understanding the Whole Bible by Dr. Jonathan Welton
    Whose Right It Is by Kelly Varner
    10 Popular Prophecy Myths Exposed and Answered by Gary DeMar

Ezekiel 36–38 (Gog and Magog)

Why the End of the World Is Not in Your Future by Gary DeMar
The Gog and Magog End-Time Alliance: Israel, Russia, and Syria in Bible Prophecy

The Left Behind Series Reexamined

Left Behind: Separating Fact from Fiction by Gary DeMar

Dating the Writing of the Book of Revelation

Before Jerusalem Fell by Kenneth Gentry
The Early Church and the End of the World by Gary DeMar and Francis Gumerlock

The Destruction of Jerusalem

Josephus: The Complete Works
The Destruction of Jerusalem by George Peter Holford
Before Jerusalem Fell by Kenneth Gentry
The Early Church and the End of the World by Gary DeMar

The antichrist

The Man of Sin of 2 Thessalonians 2 by John L. Bray
The Beast of Revelation Identified by Kenneth Gentry

Commentaries on the Book of Revelation

Understanding the Seven Churches of Revelation by Dr. Jonathan Welton
The Art of Revelation by Dr. Jonathan Welton
The Great Tribulation by David Chilton
Days of Vengeance by David Chilton
Commentary on Revelation by Gordon Fee
The Book of Revelation Made Easy by Kenneth Gentry
Navigating the Book of Revelation by Kenneth Gentry
Revelation for Everyone by N. T. Wright

The Kingdom

Rediscovering the Kingdom by Myles Munroe
When God Became King by N. T. Wright
Understanding the Whole Bible by Dr. Jonathan Welton

BIBLIOGRAPHY

Bray, John L. The Man of Sin of 2 Thessalonians 2, Lakeland, Florida: the Author, August, 1997.

Chilton, David. *The Days of Vengeance: An Exposition of the Book of Revelation*. Horn Lake, Mississippi: Dominion Press, 2006.

———. *The Great Tribulation*. Tyler, Texas: Institute for Christian Economics, 1997.

DeMar, Gary. *Is Jesus Coming Soon?* Powder Springs, Georgia: American Vision, 2006.

———. *Last Days Madness: Obsession of the Modern Church*. Atlanta: American Vision, 1999.

———. *Left Behind: Separating Fact from Fiction*. Powder Springs, Georgia: American Vision, 2009.

———. *The Gog and Magog End-Time Alliance: Israel, Russia, and Syria in Bible Prophecy*. Powder Springs, Georgia: American Vision, 2016.

———. *Wars and Rumors of Wars*. Powder Springs, Georgia: American Vision, 2017.

———. *Why the End of the World Is Not in Your Future*. Powder Springs, Georgia: American Vision, 2008.

DeMar, Gary and Francis X. Gumerlock. *The Early Church and the End of the World*. Powder Springs, Georgia: American Vision, 2006.

Eberle, Harold, and Martin Trench. *Victorious Eschatology*. Yakima, Washington: Worldcast Publishing, 2007.

Fee, Gordon. *Commentary on Revelation*. Eugene, Oregon: Cascade Books, 2011.

Gentry, Kenneth. *The Beast of Revelation Identified.* http://www.forerunner.com/beast/X0002_Gentry_-_Beast_of_Re.html, September 2008.

———. *The Beast of Revelation.* Powder Springs, Georgia: American Vision, 2002.

———. *The Book of Revelation Made Easy: You Can Understand Bible Prophecy.* Powder Springs, Georgia: American Vision Press, 2010.

———. *Navigating the Book of Revelation: Special Studies on Important Issues.* Fountain Inn, South Carolina: GoodBirth Ministries, 2010

———. *The Olivet Discourse Made Easy.* Draper, Virginia: Apologetics Group.com, 2010

———. *Before Jerusalem Fell: Dating the Book of Revelation.* Fountain Inn, South Carolina: Victorious Hope Publishing, 2010

Holford, George Peter. *The Destruction of Jerusalem.* Covenant Media Press, July 2001.

Hunt, Dave. *Countdown to the Second Coming.* www.thebereancall.org. April 19, 2012.

Josephus, Flavius. *The Wars of the Jews or History of the Destruction of Jerusalem.* http://www.ccel.org/j/josephus/works/war-pref.htm.

LaHaye, Tim F. *No Fear of the Storm: Why Christians Will Escape All the Tribulation.* Sisters, Oregon: Multnomah Books, 1994.

Pagels, Elaine H. *The Gnostic Gospels.* London: Phoenix, 2006.

Russell, Bertrand. *Why I Am Not a Christian.* New York: Simon & Schuster Inc., 1957.

Sproul, R. C. *The Last Days According to Jesus.* Ada, Michigan: Baker Books, 1998.

Varner, Kelley. *Whose Right It Is: A Handbook of Covenantal Theology.* Shippensburg, Pennsylvania: Destiny Image Publishers, 1995.

Welton, Jonathan. *Raptureless: An Optimistic Guide to the End of the World.* Rochester, New York: Welton Academy, 2013.

———. *Understanding the Whole Bible*. Rochester: New York: Jon Welton Ministries, 2014.

———. *The Art of Revelation*. Rochester, New York: Welton Academy, 2017.

———. *Understanding the Seven Churches of Revelation*. Rochester, NY, Welton Academy, 2015.

Whisenant, Edgar C. *88 Reasons Why the Rapture Will Be in 1988 / On Borrowed Time*. Nashville: World Bible Society, 1988.

———. *And Now the Earth's Destruction by Fire, Nuclear Bomb Fire*. Little Rock, Arkansas, the Author, 1994.

———. *23 Reasons Why a Pre-tribulation Rapture Looks Like It Will Occur on Rosh-Hashanah 1993*. Little Rock, Arkansas, the Author, 1993.

Whisenant, Edgar C. and Greg Brewer. *The Final Shout: Rapture Report 1989*, Nashville: World Bible Society, 1989.

Wright, N. T. *Revelation for Everyone*. Louisville, Kentucky: Westminster John Knox Press, 2011.

———. *Surprised by Hope*. New York: HarperCollins Publishers, 2008.

Unlock the Last Days, one card at a time

the card set for all teachers of the Word of God

BC CARDS — FIRST EDITION

Visit

BC CARDS

WWW.BETTERCOVENANT.CARDS

right now!

HINT: USE PROMO CODE "JESUSWINS" AT CHECKOUT